# Joint Military Intelligence College

April 2002

# THE CREATION OF THE NATIONAL IMAGERY AND MAPPING AGENCY: CONGRESS'S ROLE AS OVERSEER

*Occasional Paper Number Nine*

*The Joint Military Intelligence College supports and encourages research on intelligence issues that distills lessons and improves support to policy-level and operational consumers*

This series of Occasional Papers presents the work of faculty, students and others whose research on intelligence issues is supported or otherwise encouraged by the Joint Military Intelligence College through its Office of Applied Research. Occasional Papers are distributed to Department of Defense schools and to the Intelligence Community, and unclassified papers are available to the public through the National Technical Information Service (*www.ntis.gov*). Selected papers are also available through the U.S. Government Printing Office (*www.gpo.gov*).

Proposed manuscripts for these papers are submitted for consideration to the Applied Research Editorial Board. Papers undergo review by senior officials in Defense, Intelligence and occasionally civilian academic or business communities. Manuscripts or requests for additional copies of Occasional Papers should be addressed to Defense Intelligence Agency, Joint Military Intelligence College, Office of Applied Research, MCE, Bolling AFB, Washington, DC 20340-5100.

*Russell.Swenson@dia.mil, Editor*

*Occasional Paper Number Nine*

# THE CREATION OF THE
# NATIONAL IMAGERY AND MAPPING AGENCY:
# CONGRESS'S ROLE AS OVERSEER

by Anne Daugherty Miles, Ph.D.

**JOINT MILITARY INTELLIGENCE COLLEGE**
**WASHINGTON, DC**
**April 2002**

# CONTENTS

# PREFACE

In October 2000, the National Imagery and Mapping Agency (NIMA) celebrated its fourth anniversary. That occasion marked a significant milestone for the newest member of the Intelligence Community. In the previous four years the leaders and people of NIMA had established an identity and culture for the agency and had defined and refined its vision and strategy. That is not to say that there are no more challenges for this organization. Like all government agencies, NIMA faces issues of downsizing and outsourcing, modernization, transformation and integration. However, in view of the agency's customer-sensitive plans for meeting these challenges, at the Agency's fourth annual customer conference General Henry H. Shelton, Chairman, Joint Chiefs of Staff, remarked, "NIMA has established itself as a key component in arming decisionmakers and operators with superior information and knowledge... NIMA's customer focus is the big reason that you've been such a success story in the four short years of your existence as a separate agency."

During the spring and summer of 1995, I served as executive secretary of what was then known as the NIA (National Imagery Agency) Steering Group, as well as coordinator of various NIA Working Groups. I was in a unique position to observe the processes and politics that led to the decision to establish NIMA. Thereafter, I led the Integration Team during the implementation period from December 1995 until NIMA stand-up in October 1996. NIMA was formed from eight different agencies from throughout the Department of Defense and the Intelligence Community. At the outset, NIMA leadership decided that above all else, the quality and timeliness of service to customers would not fail during transition. This meant "protecting" imagery intelligence and mapping production processes from the bureaucratic blizzard of new policies and procedures that come with establishing a new organization (literally hundreds of policies had to be reviewed and either disestablished or modified, and the streamlining process still goes on today). But perhaps the most daunting task was to begin the process of creating a NIMA culture and identity.

In December 2000, the congressionally-mandated independent NIMA Commission found that "NIMA is an essential component of U.S. national security and a key to information dominance." This agency has come a long way in a short time. But in December 1995, the future of this agency was dependent on the approval of the U.S. Congress. *The Creation of NIMA: Congress's Role as Overseer* provides an accurate and detailed look at the "behind the scenes" roles played by NIMA leaders, other members of the executive branch, and most interestingly, the role of the U.S. Congress and its various oversight committees. This paper provides government leaders and students of government with a primer on "how things get done" so that they may have a greater appreciation for the complex relationships within and between the executive and legislative branches.

*David A. Broadhurst*
*Director, National Imagery and Mapping College*

# FOREWORD

Although several articles have been written on the creation of the National Imagery and Mapping Agency (NIMA) from the executive branch's perspective, none have chronicled the attendant debate on Capitol Hill. "Creating the National Imagery and Mapping Agency: A Studies Roundtable," is the most comprehensive of those articles, being based on a discussion in November 1997 between the editorial board of *Studies in Intelligence* and key participants of the NIMA implementation team.[1] That article provided a starting point for the present case study of congressional decisionmaking in the intelligence arena, which focuses on the struggle in Congress, rather than in the executive branch.

The present monograph may be characterized as a case study of congress's role as overseer of the U.S. Intelligence Community. A case study can follow an intelligence issue in Congress on a day-to-day basis, offering a perspective that goes beyond textbook descriptions of procedure to illustrate the human dynamics of the decisionmaking process. Thus, a case study offers the advantage of depth and detail, but only one case does not provide a basis for generalization. Works that do offer a more theoretical overview based on many cases provide a context within which to judge whether elements of a particular case are usual or unusual. Thus, it is has become the norm in academic treatments to pair the general with the specific. Eric Redman's, *The Dance of Legislation*, is a classic example.[2] Redman's story focuses on the creation of the National Health Service Corps in the early 1970s and has been used to augment textbooks about Congress in countless classrooms across the country since its publication in 1973. Similarly, Birnbaum and Murray's more recent *Showdown at Gucci Gulch* details the passage of the Tax Reform Act of 1986 and has also become a common textbook supplement in courses on the Congress.[3] Unfortunately, in-depth case studies of congressional decisionmaking on intelligence issues are too few to have resulted in a comprehensive textbook offering a theoretical context for this decisionmaking.

The case study presented here illustrates the combination of personality and process that resulted in the establishment of NIMA in 1996. It has been written specifically for those who are studying Congress and the U.S. Intelligence Community. It highlights the role of the House and Senate Intelligence Committees and how those committees interact with other committees—most specifically the Armed Services Committees. It augments the few good sources that exist on this very narrow subject—the most important being Frank Smist's *Congress Oversees the U.S. Intelligence Community*,[4] Loch Johnson's *A Season of Inquiry*[5] and Britt Snider's *Sharing Secrets with Lawmakers*.[6] This case should

---

[1] "Creating the National Imagery and Mapping Agency: A Studies Roundtable," in *Studies in Intelligence* 42, 1 (1998): 39-49.

[2] Eric Redman, *Dance of Legislation* (NY: Simon and Schuster, 1973).

[3] Jeffrey H. Birnbaum and Alan S. Murray, *Showdown at Gucci Gulch* (NY: Vintage Books, 1987).

[4] Frank Smist, *Congress Oversees the U.S. Intelligence Community*: 1947-1994, Second Edition (Knoxville: University of Tennessee, 1994).

[5] Loch Johnson, *A Season of Inquiry: The Senate Intelligence Investigation* (Lexington: University of Kentucky Press, 1985).

[6] L. Britt Snider, *Sharing Secrets with Lawmakers* (Washington D.C.: Center for the Study of Intelligence, 1997).

be read with that context in mind, and any generalizations based on this one case should be made with extreme care.

Although oversight is often associated with confrontational investigation into suspected wrongdoing, the reality is that most oversight is routine and occurs within the normal authorization and appropriation process.[7] Legislative oversight is designed to ensure that Congress has the information it needs to develop legislation, monitor the implementation of public policy and disclose to the public how its government is performing. Oversight objectives vary. "The focus may be on promoting administrative efficiency and economy in government, protecting and supporting favored policies and programs, airing an administration's failures or wrongdoing, or its achievements, publicizing a particular member's or committee's goals, reasserting congressional authority vis-a-vis the executive branch, or assuaging the interests of pressure groups."[8] Oversight continues after a law is passed. According to Senator Phil Gramm (R-TX) "Congress's duty didn't end in passing this law. We have to make sure the law works."[9] In the NIMA case, Congress adopted its role as overseer in first determining whether the concept of NIMA was a good one, and it has continued to exercise its oversight responsibilities in the years since its establishment to ensure that the agency evolved in the way envisioned by its creators.

Beyond the personality and politics evident in this case, it is important to recognize the fact that congressional members and staffers take their oversight responsibilities very seriously. The creation of NIMA was an executive branch proposal that was scrutinized from every angle on the Hill. The concerns of a myriad of interested parties—to include federal workers, NIMA customers, NIMA components, constituents, the White House Chief of Staff—were all funneled into 13 different congressional committees—to be resolved primarily by the Intelligence and Armed Services committees. The beauty of Congress is its ability to weigh the merits of a host of special interests in a way that satisfies a majority of its members and hopefully results in good public policy. In its role as overseer it must be skeptical, demanding justification for each and every proposal. To continue its role as overseer, to stay a part of the process, "to have a seat at the table," congressional committees must have jurisdiction over an executive branch agency or program. As may be seen in this case, jurisdictional concerns were paramount largely because Members sincerely wanted to play a part in guiding NIMA's evolution over time.

---

[7] See Walter Oleszek, *Congressional Procedures and the Policy Process* (Washington D.C.: CQ Press, 1989), 266-272 for a comprehensive list of oversight techniques.

[8] Oleszek, 266.

[9] Roger Davidson and W. Oleszek, *Congress and Its Members* (Washington D.C.: CQ Press, 2000), 324.

# THE CREATION OF NIMA:
# CONGRESS'S ROLE AS OVERSEER

*Mr. Chairman and Members of the Committee... we can no longer afford redundant capabilities in several different agencies.... I will move immediately to consolidate the management of all imagery collection, analysis, and distribution. In my judgment both effectiveness and economy can be improved by managing imagery in a manner similar to the National Security Agency's organization for signals intelligence.*[10]

— Director of Central Intelligence (DCI) Candidate John Deutch

## WHY NIMA?

The consolidation of imagery promised by John Deutch during his testimony to the SSCI, in his confirmation hearings for the position of Director of Central Intelligence, was a direct reference to the concept of a National Imagery and Mapping Agency. Deutch agreed with those who wanted to assemble all or part of as many as eight agencies or programs into a single, focused imagery agency. The pieces to be assembled would include:

■ Defense Mapping Agency (DMA),
■ Central Intelligence Agency's National Photographic Interpretation Center (NPIC),
■ Central Imagery Office (CIO),
■ National Reconnaissance Office (NRO) Imagery Processing,
■ Defense Airborne Reconnaissance Office (DARO),
■ Defense Intelligence Agency's Photographic Interpretation Section (DIA/PGX),
■ Defense Dissemination Program Office (DDPO) and
■ Central Intelligence Agency's imagery-related elements/programs.

According to Leo Hazlewood, then CIA Deputy Director for Science and Technology, Deutch's announcement "came as a complete surprise to the bureaucracy at Langley" (CIA headquarters).[11] Senior leadership there thought the NIMA idea had died in the early 1990s, due to Chairman, Joint Chiefs of Staff (CJCS) General Colin Powell's opposition. Deutch brought the idea back to life in April 1995.

The idea for such an agency seems to have been first put into writing as a conclusion in the Burnett Panel Report.[12] The panel, established in 1992 by DCI Gates, was charged

---

[10] U.S. Congress, Senate, Select Committee on Intelligence, Confirmation Hearings of John Deutch, 94th Congress, 1st sess., 26 April 1995, 1, 8 and 9.

[11] Leo Hazlewood, Deputy Director, NIMA Implementation Team, interview by the author, 6 October 2000.

[12] The Burnett Panel was made up of active or retired senior military officers according to Greg Jay, Contractor with Booz, Allen and Hamilton, in "Creating the National Imagery and Mapping Agency: A Studies Roundtable," in *Studies in Intelligence* 42, no. 1 (1998): 42. According to Hazlewood, DCI Gates handpicked its members. It was one of 15-17 task forces created by Gates when he first became DCI. Hazlewood interview.

with examining the structure guiding the Intelligence Community's imagery assets and one of its recommendations was to integrate imagery and mapping.[13] Reorganization of the entire defense establishment was a popular idea in the early 1990s, following the fall of the Berlin Wall in 1989.[14] At about the same time, reorganization of the Intelligence Community was popular in the aftermath of DESERT STORM. Leo Hazlewood attributes the attractiveness of a NIMA concept to three particular problems encountered during that operation: jurisdictional disputes over the dissemination of imagery, competing tasking authorities, and confusion over who owned NPIC (CIA or DIA).[15] The Burnett Panel sought solutions to these problems and many others. Its recommendation for an agency like NIMA was based on a conceptual seed planted by Keith Hall, the person Leo Hazlewood calls the "intellectual father" of the NIMA concept. As Deputy Assistant Secretary of Defense for Intelligence and Security at the time the Panel was deliberating, Hall sold his idea to several panel members. In fact, the FY 1992 Intelligence Authorization Bill recommended establishing a National Imagery Agency (NIA) in line with the Burnett Panel recommendation. The timing was not right, however, in either the executive or legislative branches, for reasons discussed later in this article. It would take another four years and the notoriety of problems associated with the Central Imagery Office (CIO) to "make NIMA happen."

NIMA was created near the end of the 104th Congress—a Congress in which there were numerous proposals to reorganize the U.S. Intelligence Community (IC). An intensive review undertaken by the House Permanent Select Committee on Intelligence (HPSCI) culminated in a lengthy document titled *IC21: Intelligence Community in the 21st Century* and legislation called the *Intelligence Community Act* (H.R. 3237), reported to the floor of the House on 13 June 1996. Also in 1996, the Senate Select Committee on Intelligence (SSCI) was engaged in its own hearings, building upon an extensive set of interviews carried out in the early 1990s. The Commission on the Roles and Capabilities of the U.S. Intelligence Community, known as the Aspin-Brown Commission, was also winding up a year-long investigation along these same lines. The Aspin-Brown Commission presented its report to the SSCI in formal testimony on 6 March 1996;[16] the SSCI Chairman and Vice Chairman, Senators Specter and Kerrey, introduced the report to the Senate as S. 1593 on the same day.

In all of these reviews, one theme predominated: "the extent to which the Nation's various intelligence agencies should be managed more *corporately*. DCI's have had coordinative mechanisms... but they have not created a corporate body with more tightly controlled

---

[13] According to Leo Hazlewood in "Creating the National Imagery and Mapping Agency: A Studies Roundtable," in *Studies in Intelligence* 42, no. 1 (1998): 42. Article cited hereafter as "Creation of NIMA."

[14] The "peace dividend" was widely viewed as an opportunity to cut defense spending and increase spending on domestic issues such as education. Thus, a variety of terms such as *downsizing, restructuring, streamlining, consolidation of assets*, and so on, came to be associated with budget cutting. These ideas fit nicely with Vice President Gore's *Reinventing Government* initiatives. Many reorganization studies, undertaken in the name of greater efficiency, also had budget cutting goals as a high priority.

[15] Hazlewood interview.

[16] Harold Brown, Warren Rudman, and Les Aspin, *Preparing for the 21st Century: An Appraisal of U.S. Intelligence* (Washington, DC: GPO, 6 March 1996). The report is widely known as "Aspin-Brown."

budget execution, missions, procedures, products and methods of dissemination."[17] The reports recommended, to varying degrees, expanded authority for the DCI to allocate, allot, obligate or spend IC funds to better manage his domain. These expanded authorities came at the expense of the Secretary of Defense's authorities—creating immediate opposition by the Armed Services committees. There was a feeling that intelligence agencies had evolved in different ways without any plan—creating redundancies and such organizational chaos that no DCI could manage it well. Part of the need for an increased corporate structure was to increase efficiency, and in the process, also increase the *quality and timeliness* of customer support. Thus, the NIMA was part of a larger plan to group similar kinds of intelligence activities together in an effort to improve management of the IC, eliminate redundancies, improve efficiency, and improve customer support. Disagreement within the Congress centered on whether a NIMA would, in fact, accomplish those goals.

In order to understand the larger context in which NIMA was created, we begin with the activities of the intelligence committees in the early 1990s.

## EARLY 1990s—POWELL OBJECTS

The early 1990s found the intelligence committees concerned with how best to reorganize the community—but not equally so. The two committees have much in common, yet act autonomously much of the time. The priorities and attributes of these committees change over time and have much to do with the leadership provided by the Chairman and Staff Director. Senator Boren (D-OK) was nearing the end of his tenure as Chairman of the SSCI and clearly saw this reorganization effort as his legacy to the committee and the IC. Senator Boren was also a good friend of DCI Bob Gates and the two undoubtedly worked closely throughout this period.[18] A staffer remembers that the SSCI interviewed approximately 185 people, all "off the record," and for "nonattribution."[19]

The House Permanent Select Committee on Intelligence (HPSCI) was also concerned with reorganization of the Community but not to the same extent as the SSCI. Chaired by Representative David McCurdy, the HPSCI tackled reorganization once it discovered how deeply the SSCI was immersed in it. Despite the fact that the two intelligence committee chairmen were both from Oklahoma, they did not get along and did not work in concert with one another. The extensive recommendations proposed by the SSCI (Senate Resolution 2198) caught the HPSCI off guard, but the HPSCI struggled to regain lost ground and emerged with recommendations of its own. In a show of unity that belied the

---

[17] Richard A. Best, Jr., "Intelligence Reorganization in the 104th Congress: Prospects for A More Corporate Community," *CRS Report for Congress* 96-681F (Washington DC: Congressional Research Service, 13 Sep 96), 1.

[18] According to Gates, "Apart from the President, my most important ally and friend was Senator David Boren.... Boren and I had developed a strong mutual trust and friendship (along with Vice Chairman, Senator Bill Cohen) in the aftermath of Iran-Contra when, as Acting Director, I worked with him to build a new relationship between the CIA and Congress. He had confidence that I was a true believer in congressional oversight and that I played straight and honest." Robert Gates, *From the Shadows* (NY: Simon and Schuster, 1996), 545.

[19] A source, SSCI Professional Staffer in 1996, who wishes to remain anonymous, interview by the author, 14 July 2000.

true relationship between the two committees, the package of reorganization details was offered jointly by Boren and McCurdy—the bulk of which made it into the FY 1992 Authorization Bill.[20] The legislation recommended establishing a National Imagery Agency (NIA)[21] in line with the Burnett Panel recommendation.

Some of the recommendations in the intelligence authorization bill were not well received by either the executive branch or the Armed Services committees. The details were considered "too far reaching."[22] DCI Gates, in a statement to the Congress on change in the Intelligence Community, warned of "deep reservations" held by CIA, DMA and the Military Services about a proposed NIA that would include NPIC and DMA and Military Imagery. He said that he, Secretary of Defense (SecDef) Cheney and CJCS Powell had agreed to approach the problem "a step at a time including at a minimum, defense making changes to strengthen the coordination and management of tactical imagery programs and my creation of a small organization that will become part of this new defense structure."[23]

According to Leo Hazlewood, Gates recognized the fact that imagery problems had to be solved and was willing to place national imagery assets within the DoD if that would fix the problems associated with DESERT STORM. He remembered that the real stumbling block to a NIMA in 1992 was CJCS Colin Powell.[24] Secretary of Defense Cheney was supportive, telling a staffer, "We need a strong DCI, and we need to support these DCI initiatives."[25] General Powell was briefed on the Burnett Panel recommendations but, convinced that DMA was "not broken," could not be persuaded to include DMA in the NIMA plan. According to Hazlewood, once Powell "killed NIA," Gates got all the players together to see what could be done "to fix imagery" within the Intelligence Community. From that meeting, the Central Imagery Office (CIO) was born.[26]

The CIO was deemed acceptable by all parties in the executive branch and Congress. Leo Hazlewood stressed that CIO was an executive branch compromise that the Congress accepted as a first-step solution.[27] The CIO alternative had limited functions and authorities. As noted in the Aspin-Brown report, "most imagery elements of the Intelligence Community, including the largest imagery exploitation organization (NPIC), remained

---

[20] SSCI Professional Staffer interview. The HPSCI and SSCI offered separate bills but the reorganization effort was offered jointly.

[21] Though referred to as NIA from 1992-1995, NIA stood for the IC imagery community plus DMA to some, minus DMA to others. DMA was opposed to joining an NIA throughout this period, arguing that it was an imagery user, not producer, and that inclusion into an intelligence agency could jeopardize international mapping agreements. "NIMA Decision Brief," October 1995, JCS "Tank" Presentation, Slide 8.

[22] SSCI Professional Staffer interview.

[23] DCI Gates' "Statement on Change in the IC, U.S. Congress, Joint Committee Hearings, 1 April 1992," *American Intelligence Journal* (Winter/Spring 1992): 10.

[24] Hazlewood interview.

[25] Rich Haver, Special Assistant to SecDef Cheney in a conversation with Hazlewood, Hazlewood Interview.

[26] Hazlewood interview. Despite Powell's opposition, Powell and Gates were close friends. The two went back many years, both having been deputies to Weinberger and Casey, respectively, at the same time. As such, they met, with their bosses, every week at the "Friday Breakfasts." Both had also been on the National Security Council, though not at the same time, and had many Washington experiences in common.

[27] Hazlewood interview.

outside the new office, which had limited policy authority and no resource authority over outside elements. CIO did retain control of the tasking of imagery collectors, however, and made strides in setting standards and policy to govern exploitation and dissemination."[28] In sum, "Politics," after all, "is the art of the possible."[29]

## CIO—"A SPONGE HAMMER"

In January 1993, Senator Dennis DeConcini (D-AZ) took over the SSCI as Chairman with Senator John Warner (R-VA) as the Vice Chairman, while Congressman Dan Glickman (D-KS) took over the HPSCI with Congressman Larry Combest (R-TX) as Ranking Minority Member. During this period, a growing number of people in Congress and the executive branch became convinced that CIO was "not the answer."[30]

Its Director, Dr Annette Krygiel, described CIO as a "sponge hammer"[31] lacking any real clout because of its lack of budget authority and lack of ability to enforce policy. CIO's problems stemmed from the fact that DMA, NPIC, CIA Imagery and DIA Imagery were all outside its authority! It had real control over only DIA collection assets and the DCI's tasking committee (the Committee on Imagery Requirements and Exploitation). Despite these organizational difficulties, its responsibilities were large.

By the time the 1994 elections ushered in a new Republican Congress, some said that the climate had shifted and there was "more of a grassroots interest in a national imagery agency."[32] Leo Hazlewood recalls, however, that if there was support in 1994/early 1995 for an NIA, it was only in DIA/PGX (Imagery) and CIO. DMA, CIA and NPIC were still opposed.[33] In fact, many organizations were vocal in their opposition, lobbying Congress against an NIA (despite Deutch being in favor), and refusing to accept the inevitability of the situation, all the way up to its actual establishment.[34] Sharon Basso was at CIO before being brought onto the NIMA Implementation Team as its Director of Communications and Congressional Liaison. She recalls that the Team was surprised by "the intensity of the guerrilla warfare aimed at us. The Implementation Team was often in the middle of some tough bureaucratic fights between CIA and DoD, and we were 'the enemy.'"[35]

---

[28] *Preparing for the 21st Century*, 23. Former SecDef Les Aspin died three months after commission work began. Aspin was replaced by former SecDef Harold Brown as Chair and the final report was signed by Brown and Vice-Chairman and former Senator Warren Rudman.

[29] SSCI Professional Staffer interview.

[30] Bobbi Lenczowski, Leader of Implementation Working Group on Organization, "Creation of NIMA,"

[31] Greg Jay, Contractor from Booz, Allen and Hamilton who supported the Implementation Team, "Creation of NIMA," 42.

[32] Lenczowski, "Creation of NIMA," 42.

[33] Hazlewood interview.

[34] David Broadhurst, Director, NIMA College, Interview with the author, 27 November 2000. That helps to explain why many lower level employees in the organizations that eventually made up NIMA were unaware of what was happening at the top or in Congress. Top managers were aware, but many probably believed that NIMA was not going to happen and thus did not feel compelled to spread the word.

[35] Sharon Basso, email interview by the author, 1 January 2001.

January 1995 ushered in the first session of the 104th Congress.[36] Congressman Larry Combest (R-TX) took over the House Intelligence Committee with Congressman Norm Dicks (D-WA) as Ranking Minority Member. Senator Arlen Specter (R-PA) took over the Senate Intelligence Committee as Chairman[37] with Senator Bob Kerrey (D-NE) as the Vice Chairman.[38]

Senator Specter's opportunity to Chair the SSCI came somewhat as a surprise.[39] Senator Specter left the committee in 1990, even though he had served only six years of his eight-year term, having made an agreement (in writing) with Senate Minority Leader Dole to return in January 1993, with his seniority intact, and serve as the committee's Vice Chairman. However, by 1993, Senator John Warner, who was co-equal to Specter in committee seniority and had lost his ranking member position on the SASC, also wanted the Vice Chairmanship position. After heated discussions among Dole, Specter and Warner in January 1993, and more assurances from Senator Dole, Senator Specter agreed to delay his return until January 1995. By waiting the extra two years, Senator Specter became SSCI's Chairman when the Republicans gained control of the Senate in the November 1994 election.

Also in January 1995, DCI Woolsey's resignation was accepted by President Clinton, General Michael Carnes (USAF, Ret) was nominated[40] to take his place, and John Deutch was still Deputy Secretary of Defense. In his role as DepSecDef, Deutch was briefed by Keith Hall (in his role as Deputy Assistant Secretary for Intelligence and Security) on problems in the Intelligence Community along with Hall's solutions—one of which was an NIA.

The idea was apparently well received because when John Deutch was nominated to be the new DCI, Hall's idea emerged in Deutch's testimony, and the creation of NIMA became just a matter of time and determination. The agenda laid out by Deutch in his testimony became known as "the symphony," and Admiral Dennis Blair was placed in charge of implementing it. To achieve the NIMA objective, Admiral Blair established the NIA Steering Group.[41]

In mid-June, the Steering Group approved a Terms of Reference (TOR) which chartered an NIA Task Force. The Task Force, chaired by Evan Hineman,[42] developed options for the NIA that took the current CIO with a few additional authorities as one

---

[36] Each Congress is numbered, lasts two years, and has two regular sessions. The first session begins after an election, with the start of the terms of all representatives and one-third of the senators. The second session begins in January of even numbered years. Thus, January 1995 was the 104th Congress, first session.

[37] Charlie Battaglia, Staff Director for SSCI in 1996, interview by the author, 24 August 2000.

[38] See Appendix A and B for a list of key players on the SSCI and HPSCI respectively.

[39] The details of Senator Specter's rise to chairmanship are included to illustrate the complexity and politics of the committee assignment process.

[40] General Carnes subsequently withdrew his nomination due to allegations that he may have violated immigration and labor laws when he brought a Filipino to the U.S. in 1987 to live in his home. See Douglas Waller, "Undesignated Director," *Time* (20 March 1995): 37.

[41] See Appendix C for a brief list of executive branch players.

[42] Evan Hineman had been a member of the Burnett Panel and had argued for an NIA in the Panel's final recommendations. A 30-year veteran of CIA, he spent the last seven as its Deputy Director for Science and Technology. He was reputedly "brilliant," and a "straight shooter." Hazlewood interview.

extreme (the so-called "CIO on steroids" solution) and a highly centralized NIA with full budgetary and management authority as the other extreme with nine incremental choices in-between. Over the summer, the options were narrowed down from 11 to 3 to finally 1.[43] DIA, the Service Intelligence Chiefs and the J2s of the United Commands agreed to some "Abiding Principles," one of which was that NIA should be a Combat Support Agency.[44]

## MID 1990s—THE EXECUTIVE BRANCH PRESENTS A UNITED FRONT

The mid 1990s found the entire Congress fully engaged in reorganization issues. The Aspin-Brown Commission, chartered by the Congress in 1994, had conducted its hearings throughout 1995 and reported in March 1996 that its conclusions concerning imagery coincided with the DCI's.[45] Despite early promises that Aspin-Brown would "put everything on the table,"[46] the final report made only modest, incremental suggestions for change.[47] The SSCI began building on its previous research and the modest Aspin-Brown recommendations, with many staffers still present who had conducted the original SSCI interviews. Because the changes the committee ended up with tended to have come from IC members themselves, they were largely evolutionary in nature—and were acceptable, for the most part, to both the executive branch and other committees such as Armed Services.[48]

The HPSCI elected to break new ground, not having previous testimony to rely on, and took a different path under Chairman Larry Combest, resulting in the lengthy *IC21: Intelligence Community in the 21st Century*, published by the HPSCI in April 1996. Chairman Combest hired Mark Lowenthal, a man with many years of experience within academia and the executive branch and noted for his numerous publications on the IC, specifically because he could conduct the broad type of inquiry Combest wanted to see. Lowenthal and Combest agreed on a manner of approach.[49] The report summarized its approach by

---

[43] According to Mark Lowenthal, staffers felt that these options were "false choices, that the options reflected a broad range of alternatives but only a few really had any chance of happening." Lowenthal remembers saying as much to Keith Hall, suggesting that they had "rendered the verdict before the trial." Interview with the author, 24 August 2000. Dave Broadhurst, one of those on loan from CIO who drafted the eleven original options, confirmed this perception, saying that the NIMA Deutch wanted was a forgone conclusion." Broadhurst interview.

[44] "DCI Plans a National Imagery Agency," *DIA Communique* 7, no. 8 (Aug 1995): 1. The combat support agency designation became a big issue between the SSCI and SASC. Senator Kerrey's position is detailed later in this article in the section titled "Legislative Strategy."

[45] Aspin-Brown, 124. According to Leo Hazlewood, the NIMA Implementation Team had many meetings with members of the Aspin-Brown Commission justifying the concept of NIMA. Hazlewood interview.

[46] L. Britt Snider, Staff Director, Aspin-Brown Commission and General Counsel, SSCI, quoted by John Fialka in "Congress Set to Approve Big Review of Costly U.S. Intelligence Community," *Wall Street Journal*, 26 Sep 94, 6.

[47] David Wise, "I Spy a Makeover," *Washington Post*, 24 Mar 96, C2. "The panel labored mightily and came up with a mouse."

[48] "The SSCI was more invested in Aspin-Brown recommendations than the HPSCI, because Aspin-Brown had come largely at the initiative of Senator Warner and was thus more a Senate creation than a House one." Lowenthal interview.

saying, "Everything is on the table. There are no sacred cows in terms of organizations, missions or functions."[50] The changes proposed in IC-21 were revolutionary, far reaching, and largely unacceptable to both the executive branch and other committees such as Armed Services (at least at first, for reasons mainly due to turf).[51]

A major theme in IC-21 was the elimination of "stovepipes"[52] within the IC. The House Intelligence committee suggested more "synergy" and "corporateness" as a way to break down barriers created by too many stovepipes and warned that "the current trend within the IC seems to be one that would reinforce the stovepipe approach, further compounding problems for little or no perceived gain."[53] Thus, the HPSCI's response to the executive branch proposal for an NIA was "Why do you want another stovepipe?"[54] (In fact, the SSCI thought that the HPSCI's reorganization of the IC would create new and different stovepipes by inserting another layer of authority over all the organizations.)[55] Leo Hazlewood remembers responding that NIMA would be a "porous stovepipe" designed to improve access to imagery-derived information.[56]

The HPSCI was also opposed to NIMA because it thought that "tactical support would win, strategic support would lose."[57] As Mark Lowenthal recalls, "We thought that NIMA would 'suck up' imagery to the military with nothing left over for State, etc. It would be too hard for non DoD to get the assets they needed when they needed them.... We didn't believe that an 'organizational fix' like NIMA was the right way to tackle distribution problems associated with the Gulf War.... And, we also saw too many cultural differences between cartographers and imagery analysts for the agency to overcome."[58]

It is important to note, however, that the *House Intelligence Committee members were not united in their opposition to the NIMA concept.* While Chairman Combest, Staff Director Lowenthal and most of the Republican members or staffers opposed it as "another stovepipe," the Democratic members and staffers either supported it, or remained undecided. The Democrats were more inclined to support the Administration's position than the Committee Chairman's.

---

[49] Lowenthal interview.

[50] Lowenthal interview.

[51] For example, IC-21 recommended increased budgetary authority for the DCI; the creation of an independent Clandestine Service made up of the Defense HUMINT Service and CIA's DO; and regrouping of IC agencies so that management of all technical collection assets would be consolidated together, all acquisition assets consolidated, and so on.

[52] Stovepipes refer to any narrow hierarchy of assets. For example collection stovepipes are defined in IC-21 as "types of collection that are managed so as to be largely distinct from one another" resulting in too much competition for resources and too little central control of overall collection needs. IC-21, 22.

[53] IC-21, 22.

[54] Hazlewood, "Creation of NIMA," 41.

[55] SSCI Professional Staffer interview.

[56] Hazlewood interview.

[57] Lowenthal interview. Lowenthal was defining "strategic" as support to the national policymakers, particularly the White House and State Department, and "tactical" support as that to military commanders. Lowenthal had worked at State's Bureau of Intelligence and Research (INR) prior to his position on the HPSCI.

[58] Lowenthal interview.

# UNDERSTANDING TURF

In *Turf Wars: How Congressional Committees Claim Jurisdiction*, David King explains that committee jurisdictions are like property rights "and few things in Washington are more closely guarded or as fervently pursued."[59] Turf "battles are about power and influence in their rawest forms. They are about property rights over public policies.... Within legislatures, jurisdictions distinguish one committee from another. They are in almost every sense, a lawmaker's legislative power base."[60]

The two intelligence committees are not equal in their jurisdictions. Within the Intelligence Community, resources have traditionally been categorized for budgetary purposes as national intelligence assets in the National Foreign Intelligence Program (NFIP) falling under the supervision of the DCI, or tactical intelligence assets in the Tactical Intelligence and Related Activities (TIARA) Program, belonging to the Secretary of Defense. At their creation in the 1970s, *the HPSCI was given jurisdiction over both NFIP and TIARA Programs, while the SSCI was given jurisdiction over only the NFIP.*[61] In 1994, a third category, the Joint Military Intelligence Program (JMIP), was added to encompass joint or defense-wide intelligence assets.[62] This development caused a number of turf disputes until a Memorandum of Understanding was signed between the SSCI and SASC conceding that the SSCI had no formal jurisdiction over either the JMIP or TIARA.[63] The SSCI can and does make recommendations to the SASC concerning JMIP and TIARA authorizations, and those recommendations are usually accepted. (see Appendix D).

Within the NFIP, the situation for the two intelligence committees is the same. The SSCI and HPSCI have sole jurisdiction over the *non-defense* National Foreign Intelligence Program (NFIP).[64] Armed Services has the authority to review these programs on sequential referral, but they cannot claim shared or sole jurisdiction over any of these programs.[65] The SSCI and HPSCI share jurisdiction with Armed Services over the *defense* portions of the NFIP.[66]

---

[59] David King, *Turf Wars: How Congressional Committees Claim Jurisdiction* (Chicago: University of Chicago Press, 1997) 11.

[60] King, 11-12.

[61] *Rules of the House of Representatives*, 106th Congress, Rule 10, Section D, i-iii. *Senate Resolution 400*, 94th Congress, Section 3 (a) (4) A-G and Section 14, (a) (4).

[62] JMIP assets serve multiple defense consumers outside a single service, such as the Defense Cryptologic Program. See Dan Elkins, *An Intelligence Resource Manager's Guide* (Washington D.C.: DIA, 1997), 17 and Ch 6.

[63] Senate Res 400 from the 94th Congress and *Memorandum of Agreement, 26 April 1996, between the SASC and SSCI, Relating to the JMIP and TIARA.* See Appendix F for a copy of this MOA.

[64] Non-defense NFIP programs fund civilian intelligence activities: Central Intelligence Agency Program (CIAP); Dept of State, Bureau of Intelligence and Research (INR); Dept of Justice, FBI Foreign Counterintelligence Program; Dept of Treasury, Office of Intelligence Support Program; Dept of Energy, Foreign Intelligence Program; and CIA Retirement and Disability System (CIARDS). Dan Elkins, 44-45.

[65] Sequential referral is explained, in detail, later in this article.

[66] Defense NFIP Programs include: General Defense Intelligence Program (GDIP), Consolidated Cryptologic Program (CCP), DoD Foreign Counterintelligence Programs (FCIP), NIMA Program (NIMAP), National Reconnaissance Program (NRP), and the Specialized DoD Reconnaissance Activities. Elkins, 44-45.

Thus, in 1995, since the House National Security Committee[67] shared jurisdiction with the HPSCI for all defense intelligence programs, it was important that the NIMA concept be supported by both the Intelligence and Armed Services committees. Since the Pentagon (the JCS and the Office of the Secretary of Defense) supported an NIA, the HNSC had little reason not to. According to Mark Lowenthal, "The HNSC saw it as increasing its turf."[68] Since *members of the HNSC were united in their support of NIMA, the HPSCI Republicans ultimately stood alone in their opposition to NIMA.*[69]

The SSCI's concerns about NIMA were jurisdictional in nature. The committee wondered "whether all the money associated with imagery was going to go into the Joint Military Intelligence Program,"[70] and thus remain under the purview of the SASC.[71] The SSCI's jurisdictional concerns reflected its deeply felt commitment to keeping NIMA's strategic focus intact. Senator Kerrey[72] in particular, was worried that if NIMA was designated a combat support agency that fell entirely under the Secretary of Defense, NIMA would focus all or most of its energy on military support to the exclusion of national-level policymakers at the National Security Council, State Department, and the like. Without jurisdiction, the SSCI would lose important influence in shaping the way in which NIMA was conceived and implemented.[73] The NIMA Implementation Team saw NIMA as falling within the NFIP and briefed it that way.[74]

Like its House counterpart, the Senate Armed Services Committee was receptive to the idea of NIMA. Unlike the Senate Intelligence Committee, the SASC had no jurisdictional issues because the new agency would fall either completely within SASC jurisdiction or be shared with the SSCI. The DoD wanted NIMA designated a "Combat Support Agency" and as such, to fall under an amended Title 10 of the National Security Act—the result of which would place it within SecDef and SASC jurisdiction but outside SSCI jurisdiction.

---

[67] The House Armed Services Committee became the House National Security Committee in 1994, and was changed back to the House Armed Services Committee in 1999.

[68] Lowenthal interview. He believes that Intelink is helping to solve dissemination problems much better than creation of NIMA did, and that time has proved him right about the insurmountability of cultural differences.

[69] SSCI Professional Staffer interview; confirmed in Lowenthal interview.

[70] Hazlewood, "Creation of NIMA," 41.

[71] To be considered a national-level intelligence agency under DCI and SSCI jurisdiction, NIMA needed to fall under an amended Title 50 of the United States Code. If NIMA fell under Title 10, it would belong to the Secretary of Defense and be outside the SSCI's budgetary jurisdiction and thus outside its oversight and control.

[72] Senator Kerrey was Vice Chairman of the SSCI and handled most of the organizational issues. Chairman Specter preferred to take the lead on the more contentious oversight issues such as evidence of IC wrongdoing. SSCI Professional Staffer interview.

[73] SSCI Professional Staffer interview, and a source, SASC Professional Staffer in 1996, who wishes to remain anonymous, Interview by the author, 26 September 2000.

[74] See Appendix J for a diagram of the Intelligence Budget. The NIMA budget (or "NIMAP") falls entirely within the NFIP on this briefing slide.

# DMA BROUGHT INTO THE FOLD

Sometime between September and November 1995, it was decided, over DMA's objections, that DMA would be included in the envisioned agency. Records reveal that DMA continued to have reservations about joining throughout 1995; however, DCI Deutch's remarks throughout 1995 indicate that he always included DMA in the new organization.[75] From a strategic point of view, Deutch would have recognized that DMA's 7,000 people added great clout to the proposed organization in terms of both budget and jurisdiction. In addition, as William Allder recalls, "When John Deutch looked at the potential for shared and complementary technologies that would be driving both the imagery and mapping businesses in the future, he saw a set of technological opportunities that could be pursued most effectively through a single set of plans and programs."[76] The target date for stand-up of the new agency was set for 1 October 1996.

On 27 November 1995, a joint letter of agreement on the "concept" to establish the agency, to be known as NIMA, was sent to House Speaker Newt Gingrich, Senator Majority Leader Robert Dole and "appropriate Congressional Committees."[77] Signed by Secretary of Defense Perry, DCI Deutch, and General Shalikashvili, CJCS, the letter began,

> We believe that the consolidation of imagery resources and management in a single agency within the Department of Defense will improve the overall effectiveness and efficiency of imagery and mapping support *to both national and military customers*. Accordingly, we have agreed in concept to create a National Imagery and Mapping Agency that would have responsibility for imagery and mapping similar to what the National Security Agency has for signals intelligence.

At this point, a NIMA Director-Designate was appointed to lead an Implementation Team drawn from the intelligence and mapping communities. On 28 November 1995, RADM Joseph ("Jack") Dantone, Jr., USN, was announced as the Director-Designate. His three deputies were Dr. Annette Krygiel from CIO, Leo Hazlewood from CIA and W. Douglas Smith from DMA. Sharon Basso moved over from CIO to take charge of Communications and Congressional Liaison and was responsible for developing a "legislative strategy" to push NIMA through Congress quickly. The team had a package ready for Congress by 15 April 1996.[78] Leo Hazlewood was told by staffers on the Intelligence Committees, "If it ain't here by 15 April, it ain't."[79]

---

[75] According to a "NIMA Decision Brief," Oct 95, slide presentation (Slide 8) prepared for the Pentagon's "Tank," proponents of DMA's joining NIMA included the Senior Steering Group, agencies and services, and some unified commands. Opponents included DMA, EUCOM, PACOM and SOCOM.

[76] William Allder, "Creation of NIMA," 41.

[77] William J. Perry, John Deutch and John M. Shalikashvili, Letter to the Honorable Newt Gingrich, 27 Nov 95. Provided as attachment to "Memo to Under Secretary of Defense (Acquisition and Technology) et al." Subj: Background Information for 16 Jan 96 Meeting," by RADM J.J. Dantone. See Appendix F for copy of letter.

[78] "Creation of NIMA," 45. See Appendix H for a copy of a briefing summarizing NIMA's purpose, Implementation Team members, and team schedule, working groups, and other background material. See Appendix I for a diagram of the NIMA decision process. See Appendices K and L for what agencies or programs were included in or excluded from the NIMA concept.

[79] Hazlewood interview.

# THE LEGISLATIVE STRATEGY

Thus, by the time the Implementation Team was assembled, it had about four months to craft a package acceptable to both the executive branch and Congress. The pressure from Deutch was constant. He ordered them to be on the Hill in December to determine the interests and concerns of relevant committees, members and staffers. Sharon Basso was the team's "eyes and ears" on the Hill. She remembers the extraordinary support the team received from CIA's Congressional Affairs Office.[80] Team members arranged meetings with anyone who would agree to hear them out. According to Hazlewood, members rarely had the time and most considered it "a staffer issue." He found House Republican Members the hardest group to schedule time with and remembers rescheduling an appointment four times with one Congressman before finally giving up.[81] It was an election year, and setting up a new agency was not high on their list of priorities.[82]

Leo Hazlewood remembers that the team had to worry about thirteen different committees—Intelligence, Armed Services, Appropriations, Foreign Relations, Judiciary (on Freedom of Information matters), Government Operations (on personnel authorities) (six each in the House and Senate)—plus the Joint Committee on Printing (for a GPO exemption, since in-house capability was needed for printing classified information). Most of its time, however, was spent with the Intelligence Committee staffers. Questions usually focused on committee jurisdictional concerns (protecting DCI or Secretary of Defense interests), how to balance national and combat commander support, the nature of NIMA's leadership structure, cost and programmatics (NFIP or JMIP), personnel concerns such as the DMA union membership issue, and constituent interests. He recalled being asked, "Are you going to take jobs out of my district?" This became a big concern of Minority Leader Dick Gephardt (DMA in St Louis, MO) and Senator Arlen Specter (DMA in Philadelphia, PA).[83]

In both January and February 1996, the team held "NIMA Days" at its offices in Reston, inviting staffers from all relevant committees out for briefings to explain "Why NIMA and Why Now?" About nineteen staffers came to the first, representing Appropriations, Armed Services and the Intelligence Committees. Staff members from the Aspin-Brown Commission were present as well. Sharon Basso remembers it was at the first session that Eric Thoemmes, a Senate Armed Services Committee staffer, became convinced that "we knew what we were doing. He had been skeptical prior to that point. From that day on, he was the staffer who successfully eliminated many obstacles on the Hill."[84] The February event drew other staffers from the same committees plus DoD representatives.[85] The team also went to the Hill to hold meetings with all the appropriate committee Staff Directors in February.

---

[80] Basso credits Bev Harrington and John Mossman at CIA. Bev, in particular, "had exceptional rapport with Hill staffers, and spent many hours working in the background, smoothing problems as they arose." Interview.

[81] Hazlewood interview.

[82] Basso interview.

[83] Hazlewood interview.

[84] Basso interview.

[85] "IMA News," Internal DIA Report, Feb 1996.

Edward Obloy, the team's legal counsel and Chairman of the Legal Working Group, described three most contentious issues the legislative strategy had to take into account: (1) personnel issues to include how to keep employee unions in DMA and whether to transfer CIA personnel into NIMA, (2) how to ensure both a strategic and tactical focus for the agency, and (3) who (the DCI or SecDef) should be responsible for collection and tasking. Compromise characterized the final solution to all three concerns.

The union issue was particularly sensitive because it was an election year, and the White House had no intention of alienating a key constituency. The Intelligence Community has always prohibited unions based on national security concerns, but clearly an exception had to be made for DMA union members or the NIMA concept was not going to make it out of the executive branch. Leo Hazlewood remembers that Harold Ickes, White House Deputy Chief of Staff, became personally involved in resolving the issue. Union members were eventually accepted into NIMA with resolution of the issue deferred until after NIMA was established.

The strategic and tactical focus was resolved through language placed in *both Title 10 and Title 50.* The CJCS was placed in charge of reviewing NIMA's ability to provide combat support and the DCI was tasked to review its ability to provide support to its national-level customers. Likewise, collection and tasking responsibilities were placed in both Title 10 and 50. Thus NIMA officially, by statute, serves two masters—the DCI and SecDef—and two congressional overseers—Armed Services and Intelligence.

On the floor of the Senate, Senator Kerrey explained his position concerning NIMA's status as a combat support agency, which would distance NIMA from the four defense agencies officially designated by Congress as combat support agencies. He reminded the Senate that the term was first used in the Goldwater-Nichols Defense Reorganization Act of 1986 to describe DoD agencies that have wartime support functions and a requirement for periodic review by the CJCS to ensure combat readiness.[86] Using that logic, Congress did not designate the National Security Agency (NSA) as a combat support agency because NSA serves customers outside the DoD. Congress subjected NSA to periodic review by the CJCS only so far as its combat duties were concerned. Senator Kerrey argued that NIMA should have been treated like NSA. However, he agreed that since DMA would make up the largest portion of NIMA, the SSCI would go along with the combat support agency designation under Title 10 "for the purposes of JCS review" (but only with respect to its combat support functions)—so long as the same sentence also included a reference to the NIMA's "significant national missions." According to Senator Kerrey, "We would not object to this formulation because it emphasizes that NIMA has two equally important functions: combat support and support for national missions."[87]

The team was willing to do whatever it took to get NIMA approved. According to Sharon Basso, "We did have some tension with SSCI, which felt we had put a knife in its back by moving toward larger control for Defense, but that aside, HPSCI was our only serious problem.[88] By March, Hill staffers had a pretty good idea of what the agency would look like.

---

[86] Senator Bob Kerrey (D-NE), *Congressional Record* (26 June 1996), vol 142, no. 96, S7012-13. The four combat support agencies specified in Goldwater-Nichols are the Defense Communications Agency, Defense Intelligence Agency, Defense Logistics Agency, and the Defense Mapping Agency.

[87] Kerrey, S7013.

[88] Sharon Basso, "Creation of NIMA," 46. "Serious" added to quote in email interview.

Obloy's legal team wrote the statute, legislative history and legislative findings, acting as a "drafting service" for the Hill.[89] This saved considerable time for the legislative branch.

In putting the legislative package together so thoroughly, the team was also ensuring that all the "stakeholders"[90] in the executive branch (including the Office of Management and Budget) knew what was going on. Regular meetings were held with all the players and all the working groups were drawn from throughout the relevant agencies. For example, the NIMA team briefed all the CINCs at a CINC Conference being held in Washington D.C. in February 1996. At that meeting, General Shalikashvili reiterated his support for establishing NIMA.[91] February 1996 was also when the first meeting of the Customer Advisory Board (CAB) was held. That group comprised national and military organizations brought together to provide a customer perspective to the Implementation Team. The CAB was co-chaired by the National Intelligence Council and Joint Staff representatives.

Ultimately, the most important executive branch player was the Office of Management and Budget (OMB). A "clearinghouse" for all executive branch legislative proposals, OMB had to bless NIMA by 15 April. Fortunately, by mid-April, the legislative package had been extensively coordinated within DoD, was in OMB at the time, and had the blessing of two cabinet officials and their general counsels. The final signature was pro forma at that point. Ed Obloy remembers having to take the package to the Hill on 15 April, without OMB's final blessing, although it did get cleared by the 23rd. He knew the Hill staffers were firm on the 15 April deadline, that missing the deadline would kill all chances of passage during that legislative session, and he was sure enough of OMB support to take the chance. He credits Judith Miller, DoD General Counsel, for helping NIMA through its last executive branch hurdle.[92]

## "INSIDE BASEBALL"—DAVID VERSUS GOLIATH

The jurisdictional disputes between the SASC and SSCI came to a head in the Spring of 1996 when the committee bills were ready for markup. Committees and subcommittees often revise bills in a process called a "markup session" in which the bill is reviewed line by line. According to congressional rules, a bill with overlapping jurisdictions (meaning that two or more committees have formal budgetary authority over some part of that one bill) are referred sequentially so that each concerned committee has an opportunity to markup the bill before it goes to the floor for a vote. This is not uncommon because any broad subject typically overlaps numerous committees. Sequential referral allows the gaining committee 30 legislative days to consider the bill's provisions. In practice, this can amount to two months.[93]

The Senate Intelligence Committee Authorization bill is always sequentially referred to the Senate Armed Services Committee, just as the House Intelligence Authorization bill is always sequentially referred to House Armed Services Committee (or House National Security as it was known then) in large measure because most of the intelligence

---

[89] Edward Obloy, NIMA General Counsel, Interview by the author, 4 October 2000.

[90] Stakeholders referred to leadership of the organizations contributing resources to NIMA.

[91] "IMA News," *Internal DIA Report*, February 1996.

[92] Obloy interview.

[93] See Senate Resolution 400 establishing the SSCI for sequential referral provisions. Senate Resolution 400 is available on-line at <*www.intelligence.senate.gov*>.

budget is hidden in the defense budget. Because so many bills involve several committees, sequential referral is a necessary evil but one that can play havoc on bill timing "strategies." Some staffers like to refer to sequential referral as "inside baseball."[94]

In terms of member priorities—reelection, influence within the chamber, and policy—the intelligence and armed services committees are not equal. The four top member choices include: Appropriations, Armed Services, Commerce and Finance.[95] Since defense spending is the single largest controllable segment of the yearly federal budget, membership on the Armed Services Committee has always been popular. With jurisdiction over the entire defense establishment, the immense size of the annual Armed Services Committee authorization bill makes these committees the "thousand pound gorilla" on Capitol Hill. The Armed Services committees are used to being deferred to. As one staffer reminds us, members and other committees are always trying to get a piece of that pie.[96] Because human dynamics and interpersonal relationships are so important on the Hill, it is unusual for any member to do anything to upset cordial relations with any committee—especially Armed Services!

In 1996, this baseball game (the sequential referral process) suddenly got more interesting than usual. The Senate Armed Services Committee took the Senate Intelligence Committee's authorization bill (numbered S. 1718) on sequential referral. In other words, the SASC took the SSCI's bill in order to have a chance to change it—to mark it up. This was as usual, and in accordance with Senate rules, precedent, and normal routine. During its referral period, the SASC took exception to many of the SSCI's reorganization proposals, and *crossed out all SSCI references to NIMA* (placed by the SSCI under Title 50) during its "mark." Still supportive of the NIMA concept, the SASC transferred all language establishing NIMA into the SASC bill under Title 10 and eliminated other SSCI proposals completely, particularly those that appeared to increase the power and authority of the DCI at the expense of the Secretary of Defense.[97]

---

[94] SSCI Professional Staffer interview.

[95] Davidson and Oleszek, 208. In comparison, the intelligence committees are prestigious from the perspective that membership indicates a congressman's trustworthiness and access to the nation's top secrets, but its members get little in terms of publicity or pork.

[96] SASC Professional Staffer interview.

[97] In the normal course of events, the HPSCI/SSCI always try to pass their respective bills before the Armed Services committees pass theirs. Armed Services then takes the Intelligence bill on sequential referral after the Intelligence Committee reports it out. Once Armed Services reports the Intelligence Bill to the floor (after the sequential referral), the Intelligence Committee can take it back or let it go to the floor. If the Intelligence Committee takes it back to reassert its jurisdictional rights, there probably will not be sufficient time to finish another round on the bill before the end of that congressional session! Thus, as an alternative, the Intelligence Committee can begin negotiating changes to the Armed Services report—of the Intelligence bill—and can offer the results of the negotiations as floor amendments. The Intelligence Committee can also disregard the Armed Services report of the Intelligence Authorization Bill and try to get a better outcome during the HPSCI-SSCI conference of the bill. Because a conference report cannot be amended and is not available to be taken on sequential referral, Armed Services must accept the outcome of the conference—they either have to accept all of it or lobby other Senators to have it defeated on the floor. As always, the selection of what to do will largely depend on the issues and the personalities involved. SSCI Professional Staffer interview.

The SASC's actions so infuriated the SSCI that *Senator Specter personally directed the SSCI's taking the SASC's National Defense bill (numbered S. 1745) on sequential referral—a highly unusual move!* In other words, it was not unusual for Goliath to take David's bill on sequential referral, but very unusual for David to take Goliath's bill.

In the committee report issued by the SASC to accompany the SSCI's Intelligence Authorization Bill, SASC Chairman Senator Thurmond voiced his displeasure with the SSCI over the issue of sequential referral.[98]

> The SSCI nonetheless included many of the controversial provisions in S. 1718, thereby creating a significant disagreement between the SASC and the SSCI. Once S. 1718 had been referred to the SASC on sequential referral (as the Intelligence Authorization Bill is every year), the SASC Chairman and Ranking Minority Member agreed to enter into negotiations with the SSCI to attempt to resolve these differences. Notwithstanding this effort to work out a consensus in good faith, the Chairman and Vice Chairman of the SSCI took the unprecedented step of requesting sequential referral of the Defense Authorization Bill.

The SASC Chairman's anger was also apparent in other paragraphs of the same report. His comments concerning a "Department of Intelligence" are in reference to other proposals in the SSCI bill which would have expanded the DCI's authority at the expense of the SecDef's. (Italics added by author.)

> *S. 1718, as reported by the SSCI, contains a number of controversial provisions, which the SASC opposes and the executive branch does not support.* On April 15, 1996 the Chairman and Ranking Minority Member of the SASC wrote to the Chairman and Vice Chairman of the SSCI to express concern regarding these issues and to urge the SSCI not to include such provisions in the Intelligence Authorization Bill for Fiscal Year 1997.

> In general, these provisions seek to shift a significant degree of authority from the Secretary of Defense to the Director of Central Intelligence (DCI), especially in the area of budget formulation and execution. *The bill also contains a number of provisions that, taken together, lay the foundation for the creation of what amounts to a 'Department of Intelligence.'*

> The SASC supports a strong DCI yet maintains that the DCI's function is not to act as a quasi-departmental head, but to coordinate the intelligence activities of various departments and to act as the principal intelligence advisor to the President and the National Security Council. Providing the DCI the type of authority recommended by the SSCI would seriously undermine the Secretary of Defense's ability to manage the Department of Defense. The committee notes that the Secretary of Defense strongly opposes such a shift of power

---

[98] U.S. Congress, Senate, Armed Services Committee, *Report 104-277*, 104th Congress, 2d Session, 1. (See Appendix E-1 for a complete copy of this report.)

and the DCI has not sought such authorities. If S. 1718 were passed in its current form, it would almost certainly be vetoed....

Title VIII of S. 1718, as reported by the SSCI, establishes the National Imagery and Mapping Agency (NIMA) in Title 50, U.S.C., not as a Combat Support Agency. The executive branch had requested that NIMA be established in Title 10, U.S.C., and be designated in law as a Combat Support Agency. The SASC-reported Defense Authorization Bill contains a comprehensive legislative charter for NIMA, which, with a few minor exceptions, is consistent with the executive branch proposal.

As one staffer notes, the SASC is "used to assaults from all sides," and viewed this as just another assault to be warded off. In fact, he remembered that tensions between the SASC and SSCI were high at that particular time. The two committees had only recently resolved the issue of jurisdiction over JMIP funds, with the SSCI finally signing a Memorandum of Agreement in April 1996 relinquishing to the SASC any claim to jurisdiction.[99] According to both Leo Hazlewood and Ed Obloy, Eric Thoemmes (a staffer on the SASC) was NIMA's guardian angel. Convinced at the January "NIMA Day" (held at Reston) that NIMA was "the right thing to do," and persuaded by the letter to the Hill that both the SecDef and CJCS approved, Thoemmes helped to shepherd the legislative package through the committee. He helped team members talk to the right people at the right time and calm the waters stirred up by the sequential referral uproar.[100]

SASC members may have been unaware of how deep the SSCI commitment was to NIMA under Title 50—thinking it to be a "Staffer issue" as opposed to a "Member issue."[101] In fact, the SSCI felt so strongly about keeping NIMA within the DCI's jurisdiction that members decided as a committee to fight the SASC by requesting the SASC authorization bill on sequential referral—a request never made by the SSCI before or since. This led to a confrontation between the two committee chairmen—Strom Thurmond and Arlen Specter.[102]

---

[99] SASC Professional Staffer interview. See Appendix F for a copy of the MOA.

[100] Hazlewood interview.

[101] Some programs or initiatives are considered "staffer issues," others "Member issues." "Member issues" refer to issues that members feel strongly about. For example, a member may insist upon funding a particular program and use every tool available to make that happen. Alternatively, "Staffer issues" refer to issues that staffers feel strongly about. Often, in legislation, members "go along" with staffer recommendations, especially when it is very important to the staffer and unimportant to the member. However, if a "Staffer issue" comes under fire in a debate between members, then members tend to capitulate more readily because it was an issue they did not feel strongly about. Not surprisingly, Members tend to pay less attention to, and be less ready to fight "Staffer issues." When the SSCI and HPSCI were created, each committee was designated one or two "crossover members" from the Judiciary, Foreign Relations, Armed Services, and Appropriations committees. One of the purposes for this arrangement was to facilitate information sharing between all these committees since their oversight responsibilities regarding the Intelligence Community overlapped. In 1996, there were six members on the SSCI who also were members of the SASC. Thus the apparent lack of communication between the two committees was all the more surprising. The SSCI and HPSCI lists at Appendix A and B indicate crossover members.

[102] SSCI Professional Staffer interview.

A SASC staffer remembers that confrontation and the many meetings it led to at the staff level. Ultimately, it came down to a meeting between "the Big Four"[103] to hammer out the most contentious issues. At one point, these Members met with DCI Deutch, DepSecDef White and Vice-Chairman, JCS Ralston to decide whether the DCI could live with NIMA as a Combat Support Agency under the DoD.

One big issue between the SASC and SSCI had to do with whether NIMA's Director would be military; if military, whether it would be a two- or three-star billet; and if a three-star billet, whether the services would get an additional three-star ("plus one") or would have to take it "out of hide" (meaning the total number already authorized and divided among the services). A three-star billet was agreed to so that the NIMA Director would be equal in rank to the Director of DIA, NSA, NRO and so on. However, the SASC wanted no increase in three-star billets. According to Hazlewood, DCI Deutch did not lobby hard enough for an additional three-star billet with the SASC and thus, although NIMA did end up with the option of either a senior civilian or a three-star, the three-star billet has to be "borrowed" from the service that nominates the NIMA Director. Thus, RADM Dantone had to be called Acting Director after 1 October 1996 because he had two stars, not three.

Having taken the SASC bill, and earned the wrath of Senator Thurmond and others such as Senator Stevens, the SSCI released it ahead of schedule. Senator Specter, in the SSCI committee report accompanying the SASC Defense Authorization Bill (S. 1745) is conciliatory, although he makes some pointed references to Senator Thurmond's committee report. Senator Specter makes a point of justifying the SSCI's taking of the SASC bill and the speediness of its review.[104]

> After careful review, including extensive discussions and negotiations at the staff and member level with the Armed Services Committee and with the Director of Central Intelligence, the Deputy Secretary of Defense, and the Vice Chairman of the Joint Chiefs of Staff, *the Committee voted to report the bill with amendments on June 11—well before the expiration of the thirty days of session allotted in Senate Resolution 400 for consideration upon referral.*

The SSCI report also discussed points of contention with the SASC such as Senator Thurmond's remark about a "Department of Intelligence." Senator Specter used the report to highlight the SSCI's success in protecting NIMA's national mission and to downplay its losses over expanded DCI authorities.

> According to Senator Specter, the Committee believes the consensus reached by the two Committees preserves significant elements of the reform effort and significantly enhances the ability of the DCI to manage intelligence activities. In addition, the Committee is more comfortable that, with the changes agreed

---

[103] SASC Chair Thurmond, SASC Ranking Member Nunn, SSCI Chair Specter, and SSCI Vice-Chair Kerrey.

[104] U.S. Congress, Senate, Select Intelligence Committee, Report 104-278, 104th Congress, 2d Session, 1. (See Appendix D-2 for complete copy.)

upon, the DCI will have the ability to ensure that a new National Imagery and Mapping Agency will be responsive to the needs of all national customers.[105]

## NIMA IN CONFERENCE—HNSC AND SASC

Typically, once the HPSCI and SSCI have resolved their differences with Armed Services, and any other committee with overlapping concerns, such as Foreign Relations or Judiciary, each bill is "reported from committee" and subject to a vote by the entire chamber. Here is where the reputation of the Intelligence committee and its chairman is most critical. In the words of one HPSCI staffer, the chairman has to present the bill to the entire chamber and ask fellow members to "trust him, and trust the committee" to have made the right decisions because the majority of the bill's contents are classified. Members can come to the committee's work spaces and review the classified annex to the bill but few do. Most trust the committee and its staffers to have "done the right thing." He calls the committee's role "the lubricant" between the wheels of the executive and legislative branches, allowing a secret part of the government to function smoothly in an open society that inherently distrusts any operation that operates in secret.[106]

Before bills can be sent to the president, however, they must be passed by both the House and Senate in identical form. House and Senate differences are reconciled "in conference." In the usual course of things, conferees include all members from the committees that sponsored the legislation, but can sometimes include members from committees with important overlapping jurisdiction.[107]

NIMA would normally have been "conferenced" by the HPSCI and SSCI—a process in which HPSCI committee members sit across the table from SSCI committee members to "iron out" any differences.[108] Had that happened, the SSCI would probably have tried to take advantage of the "divided House," using the isolated position of House Republicans on the NIMA issue to win its passage.[109] NIMA, however, was not in the SSCI bill (since the SSCI had, in fact, eliminated NIMA language in its FY 97 Intelligence Authorization Bill in order to gain Senate passage of the bill) and *there was now nothing in the HPSCI*[110] *or SSCI bills pertaining to NIMA. NIMA was in the SASC bill, so it was up to the HNSC to conference directly with the SASC.* Thus, with the SASC and HNSC in favor of NIMA, HPSCI objections stood little chance of carrying the day.

---

[105] Report 104-278, 5.

[106] A source, HPSCI Professional Staffer, who wishes to remain anonymous, interview by the author, 5 May 2000.

[107] Davidson and Oleszek, 253.

[108] "In conference anything is tradeable. It's like a 'congressional swap meet.'" Lowenthal interview.

[109] SSCI Professional Staffer interview.

[110] HPSCI Intelligence Authorization Bill, HR 3237, contained no reference to NIMA. HNSC Defense Authorization Bill, HR 3259, amended the HPSCI Bill and added NIMA language comparable to the SASC language as amended by the SSCI.

# A THREE-RING CIRCUS

Newspaper articles discussing committee differences referred to the dispute as a three-ring "turf battle par excellence." *Washington Post* staff writer and intelligence specialist Walter Pincus named the ring leaders as DCI John Deutch, DepSecDef John White (representing SecDef Perry) and Senator Specter. "Waiting just outside the center ring," wrote Pincus, "is Senator Ted Stevens (R-Alaska), Chairman of the Appropriations Defense Subcommittee and booster of the Pentagon and Senate Armed Services Committee. As Chairman of the Senate Governmental Affairs subcommittee handling civil service matters, he has gotten sequential referral on Specter's bill and is holding it hostage."[111]

Senator Stevens' actions came as a great surprise to the SSCI members and staff. According to Charlie Battaglia, Senator Stevens' staff never provided him with a reason for why the committee was taking a sequential referral on the SSCI's authorization bill in spite of his several offers to negotiate changes or provide clarification. Mr. Battaglia judged that Senator Stevens was using the procedure as a tool to show support for Senator Thurmond and reprimand the SSCI for "overstepping its bounds."[112]

# THE APPROPRIATORS

The committees discussed thus far (Intelligence, Armed Services, Foreign Relations, and so on) are authorizing committees and through their bills programs are permitted to exist. Authorization committees review the merit of existing or proposed programs and decide whether to authorize money for them in the coming fiscal year. The basic issue for authorizers is whether programs have merit, and how to prioritize a variety of good ideas.

There is only one Appropriations Committee in each house. The federal budget is divided up among its 13 subcommittees. Each agency in the federal government depends upon one of those thirteen appropriations bills for its budget dollars. In theory, every program is both authorized by an authorizing committee, such as Armed Services, and appropriated funds by an appropriating subcommittee such as the Appropriation Committee's Subcommittee on Military Construction.

Authorizers set ceilings for how much money should be spent on a program, and often outline conditions to control how the money is spent. Appropriators, on the other hand, must decide exactly how much money an authorized program can receive, working within budgetary spending level constraints. Broadly speaking, they are more concerned with a program's cost than with its merit. In theory, if authorized, it must have merit. In practice, authorizers and appropriators try to work closely together.

Ordinarily, the House and Senate Appropriations Committees (HAC and SAC) would have little reason to fight a concept like NIMA, if authorized by both the Intelligence and Armed Services Committees, since its authorization required little, if any, additional funds. NIMA constituted a "policy issue" and as such, would normally be left to the

---

[111] Walter Pincus, "Intelligence Battleground: Reform Bill," *Washington Post*, 30 May 1996, A 29.
[112] Battaglia interview. See S *Report 104-337.* (The complete report can be found in Appendix D-3.)

authorizers. In addition, Sharon Basso recalled that Senator Stevens, Chairman of the Defense Appropriations Subcommittee, had wanted a NIA/NIMA organization for some time. "He was unhappy with CIO and his staffer kept whacking at CIO's budget to force it to pay attention." She also remembered that "House appropriators were only concerned that information 'got to the guy in the foxhole' and thought that NIMA would be better able to do that."[113]

Not surprisingly, appropriators focused in on DCI Deutch's promises of greater efficiency and cost savings as a result of the consolidation of imagery assets and tried to discover ways in which the new agency could save money. The money issues were already resolved, however, and the implementation team considered the Appropriators to be little cause for concern.[114]

## A LETTER FROM THE SPEAKER

Despite their isolated position, Leo Hazlewood remembers that HPSCI Republicans tried to mobilize other House Republicans to "Just Say No" to NIMA in the HNSC/SASC conference committee over the DoD Authorization Bill. Furthermore, Chairman Combest and the HPSCI staff briefed Speaker Gingrich on the issue and convinced him that it was a bad idea. In response, the Speaker wrote a letter of objection.[115] Lowenthal points out that the Speaker is, after all, an *ex officio* member of the HPSCI and is therefore, perfectly within his rights to express his opinion on the subject within the House and Senate.[116] The letter was rumored to have been circulated among key Republican members throughout the House and Senate as a signal to the conference committee members not to support the creation of NIMA.

The fact that the Speaker's letter had so little effect illustrates not only the autonomy of the Senate, but also the momentum that the NIMA concept had gained. It had too much support from both key players in the executive branch and Congress to be brought to a halt at this late stage. Leo Hazlewood recalled that the NIMA team "discovered during this period the importance of reaching out to people who could contact influential people on the Hill."[117] One such person was Senator Trent Lott.[118] Sharon Basso explained that "NIMA was particularly lucky because Senator Lott was the subcommittee chairman who sponsored the NIMA legislation." As its sponsor, he had a "personal vested interest in the legislation," and as Majority Leader was in a good position to aid its passage.[119]

## CREATED "ON SCHEDULE"

Sharon Basso kept a board in her office from January to October 1996 that registered the "NIMA heartbeat." Depending on where the center of gravity seemed to be on any

---

[113] Basso interview.

[114] Obloy interview.

[115] Interview data conflicts over exactly whom the letter was addressed to. It may have been to Republicans on the SSCI or it may have been to the Chairman of the HNSC, Mr. Spense.

[116] Lowenthal interview.

[117] Hazlewood, "Creation of NIMA," 46.

[118] Basso, "Creation of NIMA," 46.

[119] Basso interview.

given day, the heartbeat grew stronger or weaker. Team members discovered interesting correlations, like the fact that the more the HPSCI disliked NIMA, the greater the SSCI support! They also learned that proposed legislation can falter at any moment, as the potentially disastrous Gingrich letter demonstrated at the very end of the process. [120]

Having survived the scrutiny of these many committees as a concept for streamlining the management of imagery intelligence, and having faced huge opposition within the executive branch, NIMA was legislated into existence in the FY97 DoD Authorization Bill.[121] The bill passed on 30 September 1996—meeting the 1 October 1996 timeline set by DCI Deutch in November 1995—an incredibly short time from a congressional perspective. This retrospective case study highlights just how remarkable its survival was. How can we explain its success despite all the odds against its passage?

*The importance of the combined support of the Secretary of Defense, Chairman of the Joint Chiefs of Staff and Director of Central Intelligence cannot be overstated.*[122] Had they not been united, the "fast track" approach would not have been possible. Their unity overcame the tremendous opposition within the executive branch, as organizations clashed over such fundamentally contentious issues as budget, turf, employee rights and benefits, and organizational cultures. Despite all that, the "big three" had decided the timing was right, and so it happened. As David Broadhurst concludes, the creation of NIMA was the biggest change in the Intelligence Community since the National Security Act of 1947.[123] Such revolutionary change probably had to happen quickly to minimize the weight of the opposition.

In conclusion, it appears that policymakers in the executive branch sometimes find that Congress is an ally, sometimes a foe. In the case of NIMA it was primarily an ally and advocate. According to Helen Sullivan, Office of the Deputy General Counsel, DoD and a primary drafter of the NIMA legislation,

> [i]t has been said that it can be easier to get legislation through Congress than through the executive branch. NIMA may be proof of that. If we had tried to seek an administration solution to the problem, having the DCI and Secretary of Defense sign some kind of charter, that would have played into the hands of the bureaucracies, and we would probably still be waiting for approval. Bureaucracies can take a look at senior leadership, recognize the amount of turnover at that level and wait them out.[124]

## RECOMMENDATION FOR FURTHER RESEARCH

This case concentrates solely on NIMA's creation, but Congress's role in its evolution after October 1996 continues. As overseer of the Intelligence Community, the congres-

---

[120] Hazlewood interview.

[121] See Appendix L for the *DoD Directive 5105.60*, 11 Oct 96, establishing NIMA.

[122] Obloy, "Creation of NIMA," 41.

[123] Broadhurst interview.

[124] Helen Sullivan, "Creation of NIMA," 45.

sional intelligence committees have a variety of responsibilities—one of which is to exercise "continuous watchfulness" over the agencies within their jurisdiction because the "administration of a statute is, properly speaking, an extension of the legislative process."[125] Congress gave the NIMA several years to overcome the initial hurdles inherent in starting a new agency and then sought an independent assessment of whether the concerns of the various committees were well-founded and what changes might be needed to support national policymakers more fully. Using the Classified Annex to the FY 2000 DoD Appropriations Conference Bill, Congress established a commission to review the NIMA and directed the DCI and SecDef to appoint its members. The Commission, chaired by Peter Marino, conducted its study throughout 2000 and released its report in January 2001. The Commission concludes that "while NIMA's transformation is still incomplete, and progress against some goals is mixed, the Commission observes progress in virtually every area."[126] The commission's report offers a useful snapshot of progress as of the year 2000. Researchers might consider using this report as a baseline from which to measure progress at some future date.

---

[125] Oleszek, 263-264. Oleszek is quoting from the *Legislative Reorganization Act of 1946*.

[126] Independent Commission on the National Imagery and Mapping Agency, "Introduction," *Report of the Independent Commission on the National Imagery and Mapping Agency*, (Washington D.C.: GPO, 2001), Section 1.5, URL: <*http://www.nimacommission.com*>, accessed 21 Jan 01.

# APPENDIX A

# 1996 SENATE SELECT COMMITTEE
# ON INTELLIGENCE (SSCI)

(Republicans shown in Roman type, Democrats in *italic* type)

224-1700 SH-211 Party Ratio: R 9- D 8

● **MEMBERS:**[127]

| | |
|---|---|
| **Arlen Specter, PA, Chairman** | (SAC, SJC) |
| Richard Lugar, IN | (SFRC) |
| Richard Shelby, AL | (SAC) |
| Mike Dewine, OH | (SJC) |
| Jon Kyl, AZ | (SJC) |
| James Inhofe, OK | (SASC) |
| Kay Bailey Hutchinson, TX | |
| Connie Mack, FL | |
| William Cohen, ME | (SASC) |
| | |
| Bob Dole, KS, ex officio | |
| | |
| *J. Robert Kerrey, NE, Vice Chair* | *(SAC)* |
| *John Glenn, Ohio* | *(SASC)* |
| *Richard Bryan, NV* | *(SASC)* |
| *Bob Graham* | |
| *John Kerry, MA* | *(SFRC)* |
| *Max Baucus, MN* | |
| *J. Bennett Johnston, LA* | |
| *Charles Robb, VA* | *(SASC)* |
| | |
| *Thomas Daschle, SD, ex officio* | |

● **KEY STAFF:**

Charles Battaglia, Staff Director
Chris Straub, Minority Staff Director
Suzanne Spalding, General Counsel
Art Grant, Professional Staff, Liaison for Senator Kerrey
Mary Sturtevant, Professional Staff (Budget)

---

[127] "Crossover" members on the SSCI sit not only on the SSCI but also other committees with intelligence oversight responsibilities. The committee in the parenthesis indicates which committee the person is a crossover member from: Judiciary (SJC), Foreign Relations (SFRC), Armed Services (SASC), or Appropriations (SAC).

# APPENDIX B

# 1996 HOUSE PERMANENT SELECT COMMITTEE ON INTELLIGENCE (HPSCI)

(Republicans shown in Roman type, Democrats in *italic* type)

225-4121 H405 Capitol Party Ratio: R 9-D 7

● **MEMBERS:**[128]

**Larry Combest, TX, Chairman**

| | |
|---|---|
| Robert Dornan, CA | (HNSC) |
| Bill Young, FL | (HAC) |
| Jim Hansen, UT | (HNSC) |
| Jerry Lewis, CA | (HAC) |
| Porter Goss, FL[129] | |
| Bud Shuster, PA | |
| Bill McCollum, FL | (HJC) |
| Michael Castle, DE | |

Newt Gingrich, GA, ex officio

| | |
|---|---|
| *Norman Dicks, WA, Ranking Minority Mbr* | *(HAC)* |
| *Bill Richardson, NM* | |
| *Julian Dixon, CA* | *(HAC)* |
| *Bob Torricelli, NJ* | *(HIRC)* |
| *Ronald Coleman,TX* | *(HAC)* |
| *David Skaggs, CO* | *(HAC)* |
| *Nancy Pelosi, CA* | *(HAC)* |

*Dick Gephardt, Mo, ex officio*

● **KEY STAFF:**

Mark Lowenthal, Staff Director
Louis Dupart, Chief Counsel
Michael Sheehy, Minority Counsel
Karen Wagner, Majority Staff
Tim Sample, Majority Staff
Mary Englebreth, Majority Staff

---

[128] "Crossover" members on the HPSCI sit not only on the HPSCI but also other committees with intelligence oversight responsibilities. The committee in the parenthesis indicates which committee the person is a crossover member from: Judiciary (HJC), International Relations (HIRC), National Security (HNSC), or Appropriations (HAC). (The House Armed Services Committee (HASC) was renamed the HNSC in 1994 and then changed back to the HASC in 1999.)

[129] By chance, Porter Goss also sits on the Rules committee. It is very helpful for the HPSCI to have a member on the committee that determines under what rules a bill will be debated on the House floor.

# APPENDIX C

# EXECUTIVE BRANCH PLAYERS AT A GLANCE

**OFFICE OF THE DIRECTOR OF CENTRAL INTELLIGENCE**

| | |
|---|---|
| John Deutch | Director of Central Intelligence |
| Jeff Smith | General Counsel, CIA |

**SENIOR STEERING GROUP**

● **CO-CHAIRPERSONS:**

| | |
|---|---|
| Paul Kaminski | Under SecDef for Acquisition and Technology |
| George Tenet | Deputy Dir, CIA |
| Adm Bill Owens | Vice Chairman, JCS |

● **MEMBERS:**

| | |
|---|---|
| Keith Hall | Exec Dir, Intel Community Affairs |
| Emmet Paige | Asst SecDef for $C^3I$ |
| Nora Slatkin | Exec Dir, CIA |
| Ted Warner | Asst SecDef, Strategy and Requirements |
| Randy Beers | National Security Council Staff |

**NIMA IMPLEMENTATION TEAM**

● **MEMBERS:**

| | **(Position at the time)** |
|---|---|
| **RADM Jack Dantone, Director** | Dep Director for Military Support, NRO; Dep Dir for Ops, Natl Sys Spt, Jt Staff; and Dep Dir for Def Spt Proj Off, OSD |
| **Leo Hazlewood, Deputy Director** | Dep Dir for Admin, CIA |
| **Dr Annette Krygiel, Deputy Director** | Dir, CIO |
| **W. Douglas Smith, NIMA Team Ldr** | Dep Dir, DMA |
| **David Broadhurst, Integration Team** | CIO |
| **Edward Obloy, Team Counsel** | General Counsel, DMA |
| **Sharon Basso, Communications** | CIO |

● **WORKING GROUP CHAIRPERSONS:**

| | **(Working Group Titles)** |
|---|---|
| **Bill Allder** (CIO) | Responsibilities & Boundaries |
| **Marna Bowytz** (NPIC) | Contracting Activities |
| **Jeff Boyle** (CIO) | Infrastructure |
| **George Clark** (CIA) | Human Resources |
| **Bobbi Lenczowski** (DMA) | Organizational Structure |
| **Tish Long** (DIA) | Program and Budget |
| **Edward Obloy** (DMA) | Legal |
| **Bob Roger** (NPIC) | Strategic Planning |

# APPENDIX D

## SHARED JURISDICTION OVER THE INTELLIGENCE BUDGET

| BUDGET CATEGORY | HPSCI | SSCI | ARMED SERVICES | APPRO-PRIATIONS |
|---|---|---|---|---|
| **NFIP** (National Foreign Intel Program) | | | | |
| ♦ CIA | yes | yes | NO | yes |
| ♦ Defense NFIP, such as the following: | yes | yes | yes | yes |
| ♦ NIMAP (NIMA Program) | yes | yes | yes | yes |
| ♦ GDIP (Gen Def Intell Prog -- DIA) | yes | yes | yes | yes |
| ♦ CCP (Consolidated Cryptologic Program -- NSA) | yes | yes | yes | yes |
| ♦ NRP (Natl Recon Prog -- NRO) | yes | yes | yes | yes |
| ♦ Civilian Intel Functions such as: | yes | yes | NO | yes |
| ♦ STATE INR (Bur of Intel & Research) | yes | yes | NO | yes |
| ♦ FBI CT (Counter Terrorism) | yes | yes | NO | yes |
| ♦ TREASURY IN | yes | yes | NO | yes |
| **\*JMIP** (Jt Mil Intel Prog -- DOD wide)<br><br>(Programs such as: DCP -- Defense Cryptologic Prog; DIMAP -- Defense Imagery and Mapping Prog, and DGIAP -- Defense General Intel Applications Program) | yes | NO | yes | yes |
| **TIARA** (Tactical Intel and Related Activities) (Service Specific ) | yes | NO | yes | yes |

\* JMIP was added as a budget category in 1993. In 1996 a MOA was signed between the SSCI and SASC conceeding that the SSCI had no formal jurisdiction over either JMIP or TIARA.

# APPENDIX E

## SENATE COMMITTEE REPORTS

**E-1: 104-277, SASC RPT ON SSCI BILL S 1718**

**E-2: 104-278, SSCI RPT ON SASC BILL S 1745**

**E-3: 104-337, SGAC RPT ON SSCI BILL S 1718**

# APPENDIX E-1

# 104-277, SENATE ARMED SERVICES COMMITTEE REPORT ON SSCI BILL S 1718

**104th Congress, 2nd Session        Senate        Report 104-277**

## TO AUTHORIZE APPROPRIATIONS FOR FISCAL YEAR 1997 FOR INTELLIGENCE AND INTELLIGENCE-RELATED ACTIVITIES OF THE UNITED STATES GOVERNMENT

June 6, 1996- Ordered to be printed

Mr. THURMOND, from the Committee on Armed Services, submitted the following
REPORT
[To accompany S. 1718]

The Committee on Armed Services, to which was referred the bill (S. 1718) having considered the same, reports favorably thereon with amendments and recommends that the bill as amended do pass.

## PURPOSE OF THE BILL

S. 1718 would authorize appropriations for fiscal year 1997 for intelligence and intelligence-related activities of the United States Government, including certain Department of Defense intelligence-related activities within the jurisdiction of the Senate Armed Services Committee (SASC).

The Senate Select Committee on Intelligence (SSCI) reported the bill on April 30, 1996 and it was referred to the Committee on Armed Services on May 2, 1996 in accordance with section 3(b) of Senate Resolution 400, 94th Congress.

## SCOPE OF COMMITTEE REVIEW

The committee conducted a detailed review of the intelligence community authorization request for fiscal year 1997. The committee conducted hearings and met with the Chairman and Vice Chairman of the SSCI to discuss budget matters and legislative provisions of concern to both committees. The committee also engaged in lengthy and detailed negotiations in an attempt to resolve issues of disagreement between the SASC and the SSCI.

**The committee has carefully reviewed the report of the SSCI (Sen. Rep. 104-258) and has incorporated the relevant budget decisions of the SSCI into S. 1745, the National Defense Authorization Act for Fiscal Year 1997, which was reported to the Senate on May 13, 1996.**

The following explains the committee's proposed amendment to the bill as reported by the SSCI, as well as the committee's clarification to the report issued by the SSCI.

**S. 1718, as reported by the SSCI, contains a number of controversial provisions, which the SASC opposes and the Executive Branch does not support.** On April 15, 1996, the Chairman and Ranking Minority Member of the SASC wrote to the Chairman and Vice Chairman of the SSCI to express concern regarding these issues and to urge the SSCI not to include such provisions in the Intelligence Authorization Bill for Fiscal Year 1997. **In general, these provisions seek to shift a significant degree of authority from the Secretary of Defense to the Director of Central Intelligence (DCI), especially in the area of budget formulation and execution. The bill also contains a number of provisions that, taken together, lay the foundation for the creation of what amounts to a 'Department of Intelligence.' The SASC supports a strong DCI yet maintains that the DCI's function is not to act as a quasi-departmental head, but to coordinate the intelligence activities of various departments and to act as the principal intelligence advisor to the President and the National Security Council. Providing the DCI the type of authority recommended by the SSCI would seriously undermine the Secretary of Defense's ability to manage the Department of Defense. The committee notes that the Secretary of Defense strongly opposes such a shift of power and the DCI has not sought such authorities. If S. 1718 were passed in its current form, it would almost certainly be vetoed.**

**The SSCI nonetheless included many of the controversial provisions in S. 1718, thereby creating a significant disagreement between the SASC and the SSCI. Once S. 1718 had been referred to the SASC on sequential referral (as the Intelligence Authorization Bill is every year), the SASC Chairman and Ranking Minority Member agreed to enter into negotiations with the SSCI to attempt to resolve these differences. Notwithstanding this effort to work out a consensus in good faith, the Chairman and Vice Chairman of the SSCI took the unprecedented step of requesting sequential referral of the Defense Authorization Bill.**

After three weeks of negotiations and four proposals and counter-proposals between the committees, the SASC concluded that, given the SSCI's insistence on retaining many of the controversial elements of S. 1718, the differences between the committees were unresolvable through negotiation. Therefore, the SASC has decided to report S. 1718 to the Senate, with a proposed amendment addressing the bill's major deficiencies. The SSCI retains the right to follow a similar procedure with regard to S. 1745. This approach would leave it to the Senate to resolve issues of disagreement between the committees on both S. 1718 and S. 1745.

The committee notes that its proposed amendment only deals with issues within the jurisdiction of the SASC, and that S. 1718 contains a number of other controversial provisions that fall within the jurisdiction of other committees. The committee has not taken a position on these matters, per se, but individual members of the committee, or other members of the Senate, may offer amendments to S. 1718 to address these issues.

The committee recommends the following specific amendments to S. 1718.

*Section 707—Enhancement of authority of Director of Central Intelligence to manage budget, personnel, and activities of intelligence community*

Section 707, as reported by the SSCI, would significantly expand the DCI's authority over the DOD elements of the intelligence community. It would: (1) require the Secretary of Defense to get DCI concurrence on the Joint Military Intelligence Program (JMIP) budget, and consult with the DCI on the Tactical Intelligence and Related Activities (TIARA) budget; (2) give the DCI authority to manage all the national collection activities of the intelligence community (including Defense human intelligence); (3) require that any reprogramming within the JMIP receive DCI approval; (4) give the DCI authority to reprogram funds and transfer personnel among National Foreign Intelligence Program (NFIP) elements after consultation with (in lieu of concurrence by) agency heads; (5) give the DCI authority to allocate and expend all NFIP funds for the National Reconnaissance Office (NRO), the National Security Agency (NSA), and the National Imagery and Mapping Agency (NIMA) (giving the DCI authority he now only has for the Central Intelligence Agency (CIA)).

The proposed SASC amendment would enhance the DCI's participation in the management of Defense intelligence activities, but would not alter the authority of the Secretary of Defense over such activities. Specifically, the amendment would: (1) provide for the participation of the DCI in the development of budgets for JMIP and TIARA, while leaving the final authority on these matters with the Secretary; (2) give the DCI the peacetime authority to approve national collection requirements, determine national collection priorities, and resolve conflicts in collection priorities levied on national collection assets; (3) require the Secretary of Defense to consult with the DCI on JMIP reprogramming actions; (4) strike SSCI language allowing the DCI to transfer NFIP funds over the objection of the affected Defense Agency head; (5) strike the SSCI language giving the DCI authority to manage and expend funds for Defense Department elements of the NFIP, and substitute language establishing a database on intelligence funding to give the DCI greater insight into the overall intelligence budget; (6) strike SSCI language giving the DCI authority to rotate personnel in the absence of coordination with agency heads.

*Section 708—Reallocation of responsibilities of Director of Central Intelligence and Secretary of Defense for intelligence activities under National Foreign Intelligence Program*

Section 708, as reported by the SSCI, would give the DCI joint management authority with the Secretary of Defense over the NFIP elements in the Department of Defense, including NRO, NSA, and NIMA.

The proposed SASC amendment would strike the SSCI's language and substitute a provision that would require the Secretary of Defense to consult with the DCI in fulfilling his responsibilities pertaining to the NFIP (as provided in Section 105 of Title 50, U.S.C.). The SASC amendment would also require the DCI to submit an annual evaluation to Congress and the National Security Council on the performance of the NRO, NSA, and NIMA in meeting their national missions.

*Section 709—Improvement of intelligence collection*

Section 709, as reported by the SSCI, would establish the position of Assistant DCI for Collection, to be appointed by the President and confirmed by the Senate. Section 709 would also transfer the responsibilities and authorities of the Secretary of Defense for the clandestine elements of the Defense Human Intelligence Service to the DCI.

The proposed SASC amendment would modify the authorities of the Assistant DCI for Collection, limiting them to general responsibilities in assisting the DCI in carrying out existing collection authorities. The proposed SASC amendment would also strike the SSCI language regarding the transfer of authorities over the Defense Human Intelligence Services, and substitute language requiring a report by the DCI and the Deputy Secretary of Defense regarding on-going activities of those officials to achieve commonality, interoperability, and, where practicable, consolidation between the clandestine human intelligence activities of the Defense Human Intelligence Service and the CIA.

*Section 711—Improvement of administration of intelligence activities*

Section 711, as reported by the SSCI, would establish the position of Assistant DCI for Administration to be appointed by the President and confirmed by the Senate.

The proposed SASC amendment would modify the SSCI language specifying the duties of the Assistant DCI for Administration by dropping a detailed listing of areas for administration.

*Section 714—Office of Congressional Affairs*

Section 714, as reported by the SSCI, would establish an office of congressional affairs for the intelligence community.

The proposed SASC amendment would change the designation of this new office to 'Office of Congressional Affairs for the Director of Central Intelligence' to reflect that this new office would not manage the activities of the various congressional affairs offices in the Department of Defense.

*Section 715—Assistance for law enforcement agencies by intelligence community*

Section 715, as reported by the SSCI, would authorize U.S. intelligence agencies, on the request of a U.S. law enforcement agency, to collect information on non-U.S. citizens outside the U.S. for law enforcement or counterintelligence purposes.

The proposed SASC amendment would (1) limit this authority to NRO, NSA, and NIMA; (2) preclude direct participation of military personnel in arrests; (3) prohibit assistance if it would adversely affect military preparedness; and (4) require the Secretary of Defense to prescribe such regulations as necessary to implement this authority and to protect sources and methods.

*Section 716—Appointment and evaluation of officials responsible for intelligence-related activities*

Section 716, as reported by the SSCI, would require the Secretary of Defense to seek the concurrence of the DCI before making a recommendation to the President on heads of NRO and NSA. The SSCI provision would also require the DCI to provide annual performance evaluations for the heads of NRO and NSA to the Secretary of Defense.

The proposed SASC amendment would modify the SSCI language requiring DCI concurrence on appointments to provide that the Secretary, after seeking concurrence, may make the recommendation to the President without the DCI's concurrence if the Secretary notes that the DCI does not concur. This modification is consistent with the SASC's intention to extend this recommendation process to the director of NIMA (a matter to be taken up on the Defense Authorization bill). The amendment would also strike the SSCI language requiring the DCI to provide annual performance evaluation. But the committee intends to include language in the Defense Authorization bill that would allow for DCI input on performance evaluations for the directors of NSA, NRO, and NIMA for consideration by the Secretary of Defense in the preparation of the Secretary's own performances evaluations of these directors.

*Section 717—Intelligence community senior executive service*

Section 717, as reported by the SSCI, would establish an intelligence community Senior Executive Service.

The proposed SASC amendment would strike this provision. The committee notes that the Department of Defense strongly opposes the establishment of a DCI-managed Senior Executive Service that would include a large number of Department of Defense personnel. The SSCI provision contradicts a proposal made by the Executive Branch to improve DOD intelligence civilian personnel management, which the DCI has characterized as one of his top priorities, and which the Secretary of Defense strongly supports. The committee is considering options for including a version of the Executive Branch DOD intelligence personnel proposal in the Defense Authorization bill.

**Title VIII—National Imagery and Mapping Agency**

**Title VIII of S. 1718, as reported by the SSCI, establishes the National Imagery and Mapping Agency (NIMA) in Title 50, U.S.C., not as a Combat Support Agency. The Executive Branch had requested that NIMA be established in Title 10, U.S.C., and be designated in law as a Combat Support Agency. The SASC-reported Defense Authorization Bill contains a comprehensive legislative charter for NIMA, which, with a few minor exceptions, is consistent with the Executive Branch proposal.**

**The proposed SASC amendment would strike the SSCI language regarding NIMA and would substitute language regarding NIMA's national mission and clarifying the peacetime status of the DCI's national imagery collection tasking authority.** The proposed SASC amendment would also provide that the Secretary of Defense and the DCI, in consultation with the Chairman of the Joint Chiefs of Staff, would jointly identify deficiencies in the capabilities of NIMA to accomplish assigned national missions and develop policies and programs to review and correct such deficiencies. The committee expects that disagreements between the DCI and the Secretary of Defense relating to the identification of NIMA's deficiencies in performing its national mission would be settled according to normal interagency procedures, with the President having the ultimate authority to resolve differences. These provisions would be included in title 50, U.S.C. The SASC intends to include identical language in the Defense Authorization bill in addition to language specifying that the Secretary of Defense shall implement actions to correct deficiencies jointly identified by the Secretary and the DCI.

## COMMITTEE ACTION

In accordance with the Legislative Reorganization Act of 1946, as amended by the Legislative Reorganization Act of 1970, the committee approved a motion to report favorably S. 1718 with an amendment.

## FISCAL DATA

The committee will publish in the Congressional Record information on five-year cost projections when such information is received from the Congressional Budget Office.

## REGULATORY IMPACT

Paragraph 11(b) of rule XXVI of the Standing Rules of the Senate requires that a report on the regulatory impact of a bill be included in the report on the bill. The committee finds that there is no regulatory impact in the cost of S. 1718.

## CHANGES IN EXISTING LAW

Pursuant to the provisions of paragraph 12 of rule XXVI of the Standing Rules of the Senate, the changes in existing law made by certain portions of the bill have not been shown in this section of the report because, in the opinion of the committee, it is not necessary to dispense with showing such changes in order to expedite the business of the Senate and reduce the expenditure of funds.

# APPENDIX E-2

## 104-278, SENATE SELECT COMMITTEE ON INTELLIGENCE REPORT ON SASC BILL S 1745

**104th Congress, 2nd Session**     **Senate**     **Report 104-278**

## TO AUTHORIZE APPROPRIATIONS FOR FISCAL YEAR 1997 FOR MILITARY ACTIVITIES OF THE DEPARTMENT OF DEFENSE, FOR MILITARY CONSTRUCTION, AND FOR DEFENSE ACTIVITIES OF THE DEPARTMENT OF ENERGY, TO PRESCRIBE PERSONNEL STRENGTHS FOR SUCH FISCAL YEAR FOR THE ARMED FORCES, AND FOR OTHER PURPOSES

June 11, 1996—Ordered to be printed

Mr. SPECTER, from the Select Committee on Intelligence, submitted the following
REPORT
[To accompany S. 1745]

The Select Committee on Intelligence, to which was referred the bill (S. 1745), having considered the same, favorably reports the bill with amendments.

### PURPOSE OF THE BILL

S. 1745 would authorize appropriations for fiscal year 1997 for military activities of the Department of Defense, for military construction, and for defense activities of the Department of Energy, to prescribe personnel strengths for such fiscal year for the Armed Forces, and for other purposes.

The Senate Armed Services Committee (SASC) reported the bill on May 13, 1996 and it was referred to the Select Committee on Intelligence in accordance with Section 3(b) of Senate Resolution 400, 94th Congress.

### SCOPE OF COMMITTEE REVIEW

The Committee requested an opportunity to consider S. 1745 because it contained provisions authorizing a major reorganization of the intelligence community through the creation of a new agency, the National Imagery and Mapping Agency, as well as a number of provisions directly conflicting with the Committee's efforts this year to make substantial improvements in the management and operation of U.S. intelligence activities. After careful review, including extensive discussions and negotiations at the staff and member level with the Armed Services Committee and with the Director of Central Intelligence, the Deputy Secretary of Defense, and the Vice Chairman of the Joint Chiefs of Staff, the Committee voted to report the bill with amendments on June 11—well before the expiration of the thirty days of session allotted in Senate Resolution 400 for consideration upon referral.

*Prior committee action*

These amendments to the National Defense Authorization Act, along with the Intelligence Authorization Act for Fiscal Year 1997, S. 1718, reflect the conclusions this Committee has reached after six years of focused examination aimed at making the U.S. Intelligence Community operate more effectively, more efficiently, and with greater accountability in light of the significant changes in the world over the last decade. In 1994, this effort led Congress, at the urging of Senator Warner, Senator Graham, and others, to establish a Commission on the Roles and Capabilities of the U.S. Intelligence Community (the 'Aspin-Brown Commission') to conduct a 'credible, independent, and objective review' of U.S. intelligence. The Commission was given a deadline of March 1, 1996, with the expectation that its report would inform a legislative debate resulting in enactment of needed changes during this Congress.

Armed with the Commission's report and enlightened by the Committee's own examination, including numerous hearings, briefings, and interviews, the Select Committee on Intelligence voted on April 24, 1996, to report S. 1718, the Intelligence Authorization Act for Fiscal Year 1997, containing a number of measures to improve policy guidance to the Intelligence Community, strengthen the DCI's ability to manage the Community on behalf of all intelligence consumers, and enhance the ability of the Congress and the American public to ensure that the secrecy necessary for the conduct of intelligence does not prevent the vigilance and oversight necessary for an effective democracy. The Armed Services Committee took the Intelligence Authorization bill on a 30-day sequential referral as they have done every year since the establishment of the Select Committee on Intelligence.

The Armed Services Committee staff was briefed on S. 1718 in the weeks leading up to the April 24 vote to report the bill and the Chairman and Vice Chairman testified extensively on the Committee's legislation in a hearing before the Armed Services Committee following that vote. During this same time frame, the Armed Services Committee was considering the National Defense Authorization Act for Fiscal Year 1997, which it reported to the Senate on May 13. Despite expressing in a letter to the Select Committee on Intelligence dated April 15, 1996, initial concerns about passage of intelligence reform legislation in this compressed legislative year, the Armed Services Committee included in the National Defense Authorization Act for Fiscal Year 1997 a number of provisions for intelligence reorganization, including the creation of a new national imagery agency and a new structure for military intelligence under a Director of Military Intelligence (DMI). They also included a number of other provisions that directly conflicted with the reform attempts of the Intelligence Committee contained in S. 1718. The Intelligence Committee requested referral of the bill to consider these intelligence provisions, pursuant to section 3(b) of Senate Resolution 400, which provides for referral to the Committee of any legislation containing provisions within its jurisdiction for up to thirty days, not counting days on which the Senate is not in session.

*Discussions with Armed Services Committee*

During the weeks of negotiations that followed, the Intelligence Committee agreed to a number of changes in S. 1718 to address concerns raised by the Armed Services Committee about protecting the equities of the Secretary of Defense and the Joint Chiefs of Staff. Notwithstanding that the objective of the reform provisions in S. 1718 was to improve the quality of intelligence provided to all consumers, including the Department of Defense, the Armed Services Committee did not want any changes that might diminish the current authority of the Secretary of Defense, who now controls about 85 percent of the intelligence community budget. The Intelligence Committee is concerned that the current arrangement, under which the Director of Central Intelligence is responsible for ensuring the nation's intelligence needs are met effectively and efficiently while having direct authority over only the CIA—which represents only a small portion of the intelligence budget—has led to problems like those reflected in the recent revelation that several billion dollars at the National Reconnaissance Office (NRO) in funds were never expended and were carried forward year after year.

As the current DCI John Deutch, who was formerly Deputy Secretary of Defense, testified on April 24, '[t]he Deputy Secretary of Defense has got a tremendous set of issues covering a much larger range of resources—10 times—managing ten times the resources...of the whole intelligence community. So to say that you are going to go to the deputy—and I am not talking about personalities—and say to the Deputy Secretary of Defense, why didn't you catch this, he's going to say, well, I count on the DCI to keep track of this and to let the Secretary of Defense know. So in some sense, if we are going to say that the Director of Central Intelligence does not view himself or herself as being responsible for the NRO, fundamentally nobody will be.'

The Director of Central Intelligence is in a unique position to balance the cost and effectiveness of intelligence programs throughout the government. It makes sense to hold this person responsible for ensuring that the various elements of the intelligence community are more responsive to this national objective than to parochial, turf-driven goals that too often typify bureaucracies. Yet he lacks the authority needed to accomplish this objective, particularly with regard to the intelligence elements within the Department of Defense. The DCI can be given enhanced authority without removing the elements of the intelligence community from the various agencies in which they reside or interfering with the ability of those agency heads to manage their departments, i.e., without creating a 'Department of Intelligence.' The reform provisions in the Intelligence Authorization Act for Fiscal Year 1997 were designed to accomplish this goal.

This fundamental difference of opinion over the need to strengthen the authority of the DCI made reaching consensus with the Armed Services Committee over its provisions in the DoD bill and the provisions in the intelligence bill difficult. However, both sides made accommodations and ultimately resolved all but a few issues, agreeing to changes in both bills. On June 6, the Armed Services reported S. 1718 with amendments that reflected the consensus and the two remaining areas of disagreement.

*Remaining areas of disagreement*

The first area of disagreement was on the national mission of the National Imagery and Mapping Agency. The creation of this agency, provided for in the defense and intelligence bills, eliminates the DCI's independent photographic interpretation center and transfers to the Department of Defense authority for processing and disseminating satellite imagery. While the Intelligence Committee supports this consolidation, believing it can be justified by the benefits of the synergy it will bring to imagery analysis, it has worked to ensure that national customers outside of DoD will continue to receive the imagery support they need. Specifically, the Committees disagreed on the appropriate role of the DCI in representing these national customers, including the President and the National Security Council, as well as the Secretary of State and other Cabinet officials and key decisionmakers. Given the administration's decision to establish NIMA as an agency within the Department of Defense, with its budget controlled by the Secretary of Defense, and to designate it as a combat support agency subject to review by the Joint Chiefs of Staff, the Department of Defense clearly will be able to ensure appropriate consideration of DoD's imagery needs, both tactical and national. The issue debated by the Committees was whether the Secretary of Defense should be able to effectively block adjustments in the programs and policies of NIMA that might be needed to address deficiencies in the imagery agency's ability to meet the needs of other national customers such as the Departments of State, Justice, Treasury, Commerce, and Energy, as well as the Office of the U.S. Trade Representative and the U.S. Representative to the United Nations. The Committee was concerned that the proposals of the Armed Services Committee would allow the Secretary of Defense to effectively veto changes needed to meet these other national needs.

The second issue that remained unresolved was the ability of the DCI to make adjustments in the allocation of funds within the National Foreign Intelligence Program (NFIP) during the fiscal year to meet unexpected intelligence needs. Director Deutch, along with all former DCI's who testified before the Committee, publicly supported this enhanced authority as important to effective management of the national intelligence community. The DCI has the authority today to make the initial allocations within the NFIP in formulating the budget. However, when unforeseen requirements arise during the fiscal year and funds are available from a lower priority intelligence activity, the DCI does not have the authority to transfer those funds unless the affected agency head does not object. S. 1718 contained a provision to enhance the DCI's authority by shifting the burden to the affected agency to convince the President or his designee that the transfer is unwarranted. The Armed Services Committee objected to giving the DCI this authority and amended S. 1718 to delete the provision.

With the exception of these two issues, the Committee believes the consensus reached by the two Committees preserves significant elements of the reform effort and significantly enhances the ability of the DCI to manage intelligence activities. In addition, the Committee is more comfortable that, with the changes agreed upon, the DCI will have the ability to ensure that a new National Imagery and Mapping Agency will be responsive to the needs of all national customers.

# RECOMMENDED AMENDMENTS TO S. 1745

*Defense HUMINT Service*

Section 905 of the bill, as reported by the SASC, would have made the Secretary of Defense the sole executive official responsible for oversight of the clandestine human intelligence activities of the Department of Defense and prohibited the Secretary of Defense from delegating this authority to anyone other than the Deputy Secretary of Defense. The provision would have severely hampered the ability of the Director of the Defense Intelligence Agency to manage the Defense HUMINT activities within his agency today and would have effectively prohibited the consolidation of the clandestine activities of the Defense HUMINT Service into the Directorate of Operations of the CIA, under the direction of the Director of Central Intelligence. This consolidation had been recommended by the Aspin-Brown Commission, and the Committee had included a provision to effect it in S. 1718.

The two Committees have agreed to the deletion of this provision and the provision in the SSCI bill that would require consolidation and to require instead that the DCI and Secretary of Defense submit a report on efforts to achieve greater cooperation and consolidation.

### Director of Military Intelligence

Section 906 of the bill would have designated the Director of the DIA as the Director of Military Intelligence (DMI) and would have created a Military Intelligence Board (MIB) inside the Department of Defense.

This Committee has previously opposed the creation of a single Director of Military Intelligence inside the Department of Defense because military intelligence functions are appropriately shared among the Director, DIA; the J-2 of the JCS; and the Assistant Secretary of Defense for Command, Control, Communication, and Intelligence. For this reason, the Aspin-Brown Commission also recommended against creation of a DMI.

The Committee also notes that the Deputy Secretary of Defense has also testified against legislation creating a DMI and a MIB.

The Committee recommends that Section 906, as reported by SASC, be deleted from the bill.

### DCI role in appointment and evaluation of national agency heads

The Committee recommends that a new Section 906 be added to S. 1745 that would amend Section 201 of Title 10, U.S. Code, to require the Secretary of Defense to obtain the concurrence of the DCI, or note the non-concurrence of the DCI, when recommending to the President an individual to be Director of NSA or NRO. (A separate new provision in Title 10, USC, would require the Secretary of Defense to obtain similar concurrence of the DCI with respect to appointment of the Director of NIMA.) This would parallel an amendment to Section 106 of the National Security Act that would be made by S. 1718 as amended by the Armed Services Committee. Section 201 would also be amended to require the DCI to provide to the Secretary of Defense an annual performance evaluation of the Directors of NSA, NRO, and NIMA.

### Restriction on obligation of DOD funds

Section 1007 of the bill, as reported by the SASC, would have added a new Section 2215 to Title 10, U.S. Code, prohibiting the obligation or expenditure of funds appropriated to the Department of Defense for intelligence activities of the Department by any individual who is not an officer or employee of the Department of Defense.

This provision, the intent of which is unclear, would have far-reaching implications for the conduct of U.S. intelligence activities, the funds for which are largely appropriated to the Department of Defense. The Administration is still studying the full effect of this provision if it were enacted, but it is clear, at minimum, that it would significantly interfere with the obligation and expenditure of funds by the NRO, many of whose officers and employees are not DoD employees. The provision would also likely interfere with transfers of funds under the Economy Act.

The Committee recommends that Section 1007 be deleted from the bill.

### The National Imagery and Mapping Agency

**Title IX, Subtitle B of S. 1745, would consolidate the Defense Mapping Agency, the Central Imagery Office, the National Photographic Interpretation Center and the imagery-related functions of a number of other agencies into a single National Imagery and Mapping Agency (NIMA).**

**The creation of NIMA would constitute a major reorganization of U.S. intelligence activities, and accordingly the Committee has focused considerable attention on the provisions of Subtitle B. The Committee believes that Subtitle B, as reported by SASC, must be amended in several key respects.**

**Most important, the Committee believes that the DCI must have clear authority to set imagery collection requirements and priorities, and to resolve conflicts among priorities. The DCI has such authority under existing executive orders and presidential decisions, but, in light of the establishment of NIMA as an agency of the Department of Defense, the Committee believes the DCI's authorities should be restated in statute. The Committee recommends that these authorities be specified both in Title 10, U.S. Code (together with other provisions establishing NIMA) and in the National Security Act of 1947 in Title 50 (which specifies the DCI's authorities as director of the Intelligence Community).**

**In addition, as noted above, the Committee paid particularly close attention to the provisions of Section 921 of Subtitle B that would define the national mission of NIMA. As reported by SASC, these provisions would have been included in a new Section 442(b) of Title 10. The Committee has not recommended changes in the wording of the provisions but believes that, like the DCI's tasking authorities, they should be included as part of the National Security Act in Title 50, rather than in Title 10. In addition, while the Committee has not changed the requirement that the DCI and the Secretary of Defense jointly determine whether and what corrective action is necessary to address deficiencies in NIMA's performance of its national mission, the Committee expects that neither the DCI nor the Secretary of Defense will use the requirement of a joint determination to block corrective action sought by the other. The Committee expects that the DCI and the Secretary of Defense will**

work together cooperatively to ensure that NIMA provides adequate support to non-DoD customers.

The Committee is also concerned that, as reported by the SASC, Section 921 of Subtitle B would have stated that NIMA is established 'as a combat support agency of the Department of Defense.' The Committee recognizes that the largest component of the new NIMA is the Defense Mapping Agency, which is currently designated in statute (10 U.S.C. 193) as a combat support agency, and that NIMA will continue to have significant combat support functions. But unlike the Defense Mapping Agency, NIMA will also have important responsibilities to provide imagery to non-military customers. Accordingly, the Committee believes it would be a mistake to establish NIMA 'as a combat support agency,' even if other statutory provisions specifically state that NIMA also has national missions. The implication would be left that NIMA's primary purpose is to provide combat support.

In this regard, the Committee notes that when Congress enacted Section 193 of Title 10, which specified the combat support agencies of the Department of Defense, Congress specifically declined to list the National Security Agency as a combat support agency because NSA serves customers outside the Department of Defense. Congress, nevertheless, subjected NSA to the same JCS review procedures as other combat support agencies but only with respect to its combat support functions. The Committee believes that it would be most appropriate to treat NIMA like NSA, i.e., not list NIMA as a combat support agency but subject it to JCS review with respect to its combat support functions. The Department of Defense and the SASC, however, have insisted that NIMA be listed as a combat support agency. Given that the Defense Mapping Agency will comprise the largest activity within NIMA, the Committee is willing to agree to have NIMA listed as a combat support agency in 10 U.S.C. 193 for purposes of JCS review of its combat support functions but recommends that Section 921 be amended so that NIMA is not established specifically 'as a combat support agency.'

The Committee also disagrees with provisions in Section 921 of the SASC bill relating to the appointment and status of the Director of NIMA. The legislative package drafted by the Administration to create NIMA provided that (1) the Director of NIMA could be either a civilian or a military officer; and (2) the Secretary of Defense must obtain the concurrence of the DCI, or note the nonconcurrence of the DCI, when recommending an individual to the President for appointment as Director of NIMA. As proposed by the SASC, new Section 441(b) of Title 10 would have required that the Director of NIMA be a military officer and that the Secretary of Defense simply consult the DCI before recommending a nominee from appointing a civilian Director of NIMA (thus implying that NIMA performs exclusively military functions) and would have given the DCI only a minor voice in the appointment of the head of a critical national intelligence agency. The SASC formulation was opposed by the DCI and by the Secretary of Defense. Accordingly, the Committee has amended proposed Section 441(b) to revert to the Administration's proposal.

Finally, pursuant to agreement with the Armed Service Committee, the Committee has deleted proposed Section 445 of Title 10. This section would have prohibited the Inspector General of the Central Intelligence Agency from conducting any inspection, investigation, or audit of NIMA without the written consent of DoD Inspector General.

## COMMITTEE ACTION

On June 11, 1996, the Select Committee on Intelligence voted to report S. 1745 with amendments. Because the provisions considered by the Committee constituted a relatively small portion of the entire National Defense Authorization Act for Fiscal Year 1997, the Committee did not make a recommendation to the Senate on the overall bill. However, the Committee supports the provisions related to intelligence as amended.

## REGULATORY IMPACT

Paragraph 11(b) of rule XXVI of the Standing Rules of the Senate requires that a report on the regulatory impact of a bill be included in the report on the bill. The Committee finds that there is no change in the regulatory impact of S. 1745 as a result of these amendments.

## ESTIMATE OF COSTS

The Committee finds no changes in the estimate of costs as a result of these amendments.

## CHANGES IN EXISTING LAW

Pursuant to the provisions of paragraph 12 of rule XXVI of the Standing Rules of the Senate, the changes in existing law made by certain portions of the bill have not been shown in this section of the report because, in the opinion of the Committee, it is necessary to dispense with showing such changes in order to expedite the business of the Senate and reduce the expenditure of funds.

# APPENDIX E-3

## 104-337, SENATE GOVERNMENTAL AFFAIRS COMMITTEE REPORT ON SSCI BILL S 1718

**104th Congress, 2nd Session**    **Senate**    **Report 104-337**

## TO AUTHORIZE APPROPRIATIONS FOR FISCAL YEAR 1997 FOR INTELLIGENCE AND INTELLIGENCE-RELATED ACTIVITIES OF THE UNITED STATES GOVERNMENT

July 29, 1996—Ordered to be printed

Mr. STEVENS, from the Committee on Governmental Affairs, submitted the following
REPORT
[To accompany S. 1718]

The Senate Committee on Governmental Affairs, to which was referred the bill (S. 1718) having considered the same, reports favorably thereon with amendments and recommends that the bill as amended do pass.

## I. PURPOSE AND SUMMARY

S. 1718, as reported from the Governmental Affairs Committee, would authorize appropriations for fiscal year 1997 for intelligence and intelligence-related activities of the United States Government, including certain activities within the jurisdiction of the Governmental Affairs Committee.

The Senate Select Committee on Intelligence reported the bill on April 30, 1996. It was referred to the Senate Committee on Armed Services on May 2, 1996, in accordance with section 3(b) of Senate Resolution 400, 94th Congress. At the request of the Senate Committee on Governmental Affairs, S. 1718 was, on June 6, 1996, referred to this committee for a 30-session day period.

## II. SCOPE OF COMMITTEE REVIEW

The committee requested an opportunity to review those provisions of S. 1718 which addressed federal government organization. In broad terms this included provisions to create a commission to assess government structure and efficiency relating to nonproliferation and a new senior executive service for the intelligence community. The committee also noted language in the report accompanying S. 1718 which suggested a lack of effective coordination on joint matters by the various inspectors general (IGs) in those agencies comprising the intelligence community. After careful review of S. 1718, including extensive discussions with the staffs of both the Armed Services and Intelligence Committees, the Governmental Affairs Committee voted to report the bill favorably, with amendments, on July 25. This is prior to the expiration of the 30 days of session allotted in Senate Resolution 400 for consideration upon referral.

On June 6, 1996, the Senate Armed Services Committee published its report (104-277) on S. 1718 and suggested several amendments, one of which strike the concept of a new senior executive service personnel program for the intelligence community. As noted in the Armed Services Committee report a number of provisions in S. 1718 would shift authority over DoD intelligence assets from the Secretary of Defense (SecDef) to the Director of Central Intelligence (DCI). Most of these provisions were amended by the Armed Services Committee and eventual compromises negotiated between them and the Intelligence Committee.

On June 11, the Intelligence Committee published its report (104-278) on S. 1745, the Department of Defense Authorization bill, agreeing to the Armed Services Committee recommendation to strike the new senior executive service personnel program language.

The Governmental Affairs Committee only addressed issues within our jurisdiction; however, we fully concur in all the changes recommended by the Armed Services Committee including its recommendation to strike all language establishing a new senior executive service personnel program for the intelligence community.

## III. GLENN AMENDMENT

Senator Glenn's amendment to S. 1718 (1) provides more specificity as to the qualifications of commission members; (2) enumerates how the commission will assess the effectiveness of the U.S. cooperation with other countries with respect to nonproliferation activities; and (3) calls on the commission to address export controls, funding, information flow, and the organization of counterproliferation activities of the U.S., among other issues. The committee voted to report the bill with this amendment.

## IV. INSPECTORS GENERAL

An earlier draft version of the Intelligence Authorization Bill contained language which would have broadened the role of the CIA's Inspector General to act, in effect, as an inspector general for the entire intelligence community. That version of the bill would have included in the duties of the CIA IG the duty inter alia to '(a) identify to the Director programs and operations conducted by elements of the intelligence community as appropriate subjects for inspections, investigations and audits'; and (b) upon the request of the Director, or his designee, arrange for and coordinate the conduct of' these reviews, as well as '(c) establish standards for the staffs and products of the inspectors general of the elements of the intelligence community.' The Intelligence Committee felt there was a need to establish a central point of coordination or accountability for intelligence community IG issues. Better arrangements exist for coordinating interagency IG activities than empowering one of the concerned IGs to act as the central point of contact for intelligence matters. The Intelligence Committee, following a discussion with the staff of the Governmental Affairs Committee, subsequently agreed to drop this provision from their bill; however, their committee report still expresses concerns over the IGs' ability to conduct or coordinate activities involving intelligence matters.

As the committee charged with the oversight of the statutory inspectors general, we have found no evidence indicating Congress should take the extraordinary step of creating a 'community' inspector general. This would be analogous to empowering the Justice Department IG to act as coordinator and central point of contact on all IG matters involving the law enforcement 'community' which, like the intelligence community, consists of various organizations spread across more than one department.

This committee has heard from a number of the inspectors general in departments and agencies comprising the intelligence community expressing concern over several issues raised in the Intelligence Committee report. These are: the suggestion by the Intelligence Committee of a lack of effective coordination between intelligence community IGs, lack of consistent IG coverage of high risk or high dollar intelligence programs, lack of effective management support and attention to the IGs and their products and recommendations, and inconsistent training and professional standards for IG employees. In addition, the Intelligence Committee noted that concerns have been expressed by intelligence officials outside the IG community regarding the professionalism, experience, and training of the IG staffs. The IGs expressed their view that these concerns were for the most part unfounded.

In our view adequate mechanisms for coordinating interagency IG activities already exist. We reference the August 1994 establishment of the DoD/CIA Intelligence Inspector General Forum (the Forum) created to ensure adequate coverage of topics and issues involving interagency functions and programs. In addition, the President's Council on Integrity and Efficiency (PCIE), comprised of representatives from the statutory IGs, has the responsibility for coordinating interagency IG activities throughout the Federal Government. The Government Affairs Committee has been in dialogue with the Office of Management and Budget with a view toward formalizing a PCIE mechanism made up of statutory IG representatives from all those agencies and departments comprising the intelligence community. We believe this would be the proper venue for coordinating joint IG activities involving those intelligence community agencies outside DoD and CIA.

The Intelligence Committee report calls for the thirteen intelligence community IGs (Department of Defense, Central Intelligence Agency, Department of Justice, Defense Intelligence Agency, Central Imagery Office, Department of Energy, Department of State, Department of the Treasury, the Military Services, National Reconnaissance Office, and National Security Agency) to provide by January 15, 1997, a report to the committees describing the reviews involving joint intelligence issues in which they have participated since January 1, 1994. Copies of those reports should also be provided to the Governmental Affairs Committee as the oversight committee for the statutory inspectors general.

## V. COMMITTEE ACTION

On July 25, 1996, the Senate Governmental Affairs Committee held a markup on S. 1718. Senator Glenn's amendment was approved by roll call vote of seven to six. The following Senators were recorded as voting aye: Cohen (by proxy), Glenn, Levin, Pryor (by proxy), Lieberman (by proxy), Akaka (by proxy), and Dorgan. The following Senators were recorded as voting no: Stevens, Roth (by proxy), Thompson, Cochran, McCain, and Smith. A voice vote then occurred on the motion to report S. 1718, as amended by the Glenn Amendment, from the Governmental Affairs Committee.

## VI. ESTIMATES OF COSTS

The committee finds no changes in the estimate of costs as a result of these amendments.

## VII. CHANGES IN EXISTING LAW

Pursuant to the provisions of paragraph 12 of rule XXVI of the Standing Rules of the Senate, the changes in existing law made by certain portions of the bill have not been shown in this section of the report because, in the opinion of the committee, it is necessary to dispense with showing such changes in order to expedite the business of the Senate and reduce the expenditure of funds.

## VIII. REGULATORY IMPACT OF LEGISLATION

Paragraph 11(b)(1) of rule XXVI of the Standing Rules of the Senate requires that each report accompanying a bill evaluate 'the regulatory impact which would be incurred in carrying out the bill.' The enactment of this legislation would not have a significant regulatory impact.

# APPENDIX F

# LETTER TO NEWT GINGRICH

27 November 1995

The Honorable Newt Gingrich
Speaker of the House of Representatives
Washington, D.C.  20515

Dear Mr. Speaker:

We believe that the consolidation of imagery resources and management in a single agency within the Department of Defense (DOD) will improve the overall effectiveness and efficiency of imagery intelligence and mapping support to both national and military customers.  Accordingly, we have agreed to a concept to create a National Imagery and Mapping Agency (NIMA) that would have responsibility for imagery and mapping similar to what the National Security Agency has for signals intelligence.  The NIMA would have program and budget authorities as well as research, development, acquisition, exploitation, and production responsibilities for imagery and mapping.  Moreover, the Director of NIMA would have responsibility for the review and approval of other imagery resources to assure compliance with standards and policy.

A number of factors point to the advantage of consolidating efforts that are now separate into a new agency.  First, imagery intelligence and mapping products are of growing importance to an increasingly diverse customer base across the government.  We need a single streamlined agency focused on exploitation and distribution of imagery-derived products to serve this growing customer base.  Second, with responsibilities currently split among five agencies, at present we are poorly positioned to leverage the tremendous potential of enhanced collection systems, digital processing technology, and the prospective expansion in commercial imagery.  Third, the revolution in information technology makes possible a symbiosis of imagery intelligence and mapping which can best be realized through more coherent management.  In the long run, these challenges can most efficiently be met by consolidation of our imagery and mapping assets within a designated Combat Support Agency.

Since early summer, an interagency task force representing the Intelligence Community, the DOD, and civil agencies has examined the merits and details associated with merging disparate Defense and Intelligence elements as well as the myriad possible approaches toward consolidation of imagery and mapping functions. The objective has been to determine the approach that makes the

53

The Honorable Newt Gingrich

best sense in view of the complicated management, technical, and resource factors that bear on imagery and mapping activities. On the basis of the work of the interagency task force, we have now agreed on an approach that will enable us to achieve the advances in performance necessary to support future requirements of national and defense customers.

Because several Congressional committees have an interest in this question as part of their responsibilities, before proceeding with a comprehensive implementation plan, we shall consult closely with the Congress on the specifics of this proposal. For example, we are fully aware that some will be concerned that centralizing imagery exploitation in DOD will inevitably result in a decline in attention devoted to non-DOD, national users. We believe the proposed NIMA, when implemented, can improve quality to all customers at lower costs, and we are committed to maintaining service to our national users. We look forward to explaining the proposed changes in more detail and addressing the many questions that will undoubtedly be raised.

We would welcome the opportunity to meet with you at your convenience to begin this consultation period. In a few days we also intend to appoint a senior officer to lead a transition and implementation team to make NIMA a reality, and this officer will assist us in our discussions with you and other Congressional leaders.

While there are many details to work out and many important questions to answer during our consultations with you, we are confident you will agree in the end that creation of a NIMA is essential to adequately posture our national and defense imagery community for the challenges that lie ahead.

Identical letters are being sent to the Senate Majority Leader and to the appropriate Congressional Committees.

Sincerely,              Sincerely,                    Sincerely,


William J. Perry          John Deutch               John M. Shalikashvili
Secretary of Defense      Director of               Chairman
                          Central Intelligence      Joint Chiefs of Staff

# APPENDIX G

# MEMORANDUM OF AGREEMENT
## 26 April 1996, SASC and SSCI, JMIP and TIARA

Memorandum of Agreement
April 29, 1996
between
The Senate Armed Services Committee (SASC)
and
The Senate Select Committee on Intelligence (SSCI)
Relating to the Joint Military Intelligence Program (JMIP)
and
Tactical Intelligence and Related Activities (TIARA)

---

The Chairman and Ranking Member of the SASC and the Chairman and Vice Chairman of the SSCI agree to the following arrangements for the review and authorization of TIARA and the JMIP:

(1) The SSCI will consider TIARA and the JMIP in its markup and will include a recommendation for TIARA and the JMIP in its formal committee report on the annual Intelligence Authorization Act. The SSCI's bill and report, however, will make clear that the only schedule of authorizations the SSCI is recommending to the Senate is the schedule for the National Foreign Intelligence Program (NFIP), and that the SSCI is only making a recommendation for TIARA and the JMIP to the SASC;

(2) The committee staffs will work together and the SSCI staff may attend staff-level conference meetings on the annual Department of Defense Authorization bill in which matters related to TIARA and the JMIP are considered; and

(3) Before a TIARA or JMIP issue is finally closed out in the Defense Authorization conference in a manner with which they disagree, the SSCI Chairman and Vice Chairman will have an opportunity to consult on the issue with the SASC Chairman and Ranking Member.

Strom Thurmond
SASC Chairman

Sam Nunn
SASC Ranking Member

Arlen Specter
SSCI Chairman

J. Robert Kerrey
SSCI Vice Chairman

# APPENDIX H

# LEGISLATIVE PACKAGE BRIEFING, 29 MAR 96

---

## Briefing
## of National Imagery and Mapping Agency
## Proposed Legislation
[Pending Administration Clearance]

NIMA Implementation Team Legal Working Group
Legislative Package
29 March 1996

NIMA

10/3/00

**NIMA Implementation Team
Working Group Kickoff Briefing**

**Provided to
Mr. Dale Clark, DA&M, OSD**

**30 January 1996**

NIMA

---

# Why NIMA?

- Accelerate the fusion of geospatial information and imagery intelligence to benefit a growing and diverse customer base
    - > Populating a robust geospatial database
    - > Developing a system of archives for primary imagery and imagery products
    - > Improving customer access
- Increase the leverage on technology, research, and the expanding commercial imagery base to better serve both imagery and mapping customers
- Enhance the consistency of training, career development and career standards
- Strengthen the management of imagery as an end-to-end process--from tasking for collection through the dissemination of primary imagery, imagery products, and geospatial information
- Increase the proponency and focus on imagery exploitation and dissemination to meet expanding customer needs

NIMA

58

# The Decision Framework:
## DCI and the SECDEF Have Agreed That (1)

- NIMA's customers will be in the civil, defense, and national communities
    - > It will be a Combat Support Agency
    - > It will also be an intelligence agency with important customers outside of DoD
    - > Any conflict in priorities in supporting these customers will be resolved by the SECDEF and the DCI
- NIMA will be placed within the Department of Defense
- NIMA will derive authorities from the SECDEF and the DCI
    - > It will be responsible to both
    - > Its creation and operation will not diminish the responsibilities and authorities of either the DCI or the SECDEF

NIMA

# The Decision Framework:
## DCI and the SECDEF Have Agreed That (2)

- NIMA will exercise broad authorities and be responsible for:
    - > Imagery policy, planning, and the development of the US Imagery System (USIS)
    - > Exploitation and production of imagery intelligence and geospatial information
    - > Dissemination of primary imagery, imagery products, and geospatial information
    - > Conduct of associated research, development, and acquisition
    - > Review and approval of all imagery and mapping resources across the USIS to assure compliance with policy and architectural standards
    - > Training and career development
    - > Program formulation and budget execution within NIMA

NIMA

# The Decision Framework:
## DCI and the SECDEF Have Agreed That (3)

- NIMA will be assembled from all or part of as many as eight agencies or programs:
  - > Defense Mapping Agency (DMA)
  - > National Photographic Interpretation Center (NPIC)
  - > Central Imagery Office (CIO)
  - > National Reconnaissance Office (NRO)
  - > Defense Airborne Reconnaissance Office (DARO)
  - > Defense Dissemination Program Office (DDPO)
  - > Defense Intelligence Agency (DIA)
  - > Central Intelligence Agency (CIA)
- D/NIMA will be a three-star general or flag officer, nominated by the SECDEF with the DCI's concurrence; DD/NIMA will be a civilian drawn from the national intelligence and geospatial communities

NIMA

---

# NIMA Implementation Team

RADM J. J. Dantone - Director
Leo Hazelwood, CIA - Deputy Director
Dr. Annette Krygiel, CIO - Deputy Director
W. Douglas Smith, DMA - DD/DMA, NIMA Team Leader
David Broadhurst, CIO - Integration Team
Edward Obloy, DMA - Team Counsel
Sharon Basso, CIO - Communications

Team Representatives: CIA, CIO, DARO, DIA, DDPO, DMA, NRO, NPIC.

NIMA

## Guiding Principles for NIMA Stand-up

- People are our most precious resource. Protect them in the near term as we stand-up this new organization. Invest in them in the long term by increasing education and training opportunities.
- We are accountable to each other, our customers and our bosses
- Focus on added value, not on control
- Authorities and responsibilities must be in balance
- Headquarters size: smaller is better
- Build a team that communicates easily and is focused on the customer

NIMA

---

## NIMA Implementation Process Flow Diagram

Features
- Customer Oversight and Advice
- Oversight, Policy and Guidance from NIMA Implementation Leadership
- Daily Management by Implementation Team Leader
- Issue Identification and Integration By the Implementation Team
- Issue Analysis and Alternative Proposals from the Issue Teams

DCI    CJCS
SecDef
Customer Advisory Board    Steering Group

NIMA Leadership

Implementation Team Leader

Legal Team
Human Resources Team
Responsibilities/Boundaries Team
Org. Issues/Alternatives Team
Program & Budget Team
Contracting Team
Infrastructure Team
Strategic Planning Team

Implementation Team

NIMA

## Senior Steering Group

- Co-chairs:
  - > Hon. Paul Kaminski, Under Secretary of Defense for Acquisition and Technology; Hon. George Tenet, Deputy Director of Central Intelligence; and Adm. William Owens, Vice Chairman, Joint Chiefs of Staff.
- Members:
  - > Hon. Keith Hall, Executive Director, Intelligence Community Affairs; Hon. Emmet Paige, Assistant Secretary of Defense for C3I; Ms. Nora Slatkin, Executive Director, Central Intelligence Agency; Hon. Ted Warner, Assistant Secretary of Defense for Strategy and Requirements; and Mr. Randy Beers, National Security Council Staff.

NIMA

## Customer Advisory Board

- Membership
  - > CIA/NIC
  - > JCS
  - > DI
  - > ACIS
  - > CNC
  - > NPC
  - > CAC/USGS
  - > DEA
  - > NSC
  - > NSA
  - > STATE
  - > TRANSPORTATION/COAST GUARD
  - > TREASURY/SECRET SERVICE
  - > DEA
  - > FEMA

NIMA

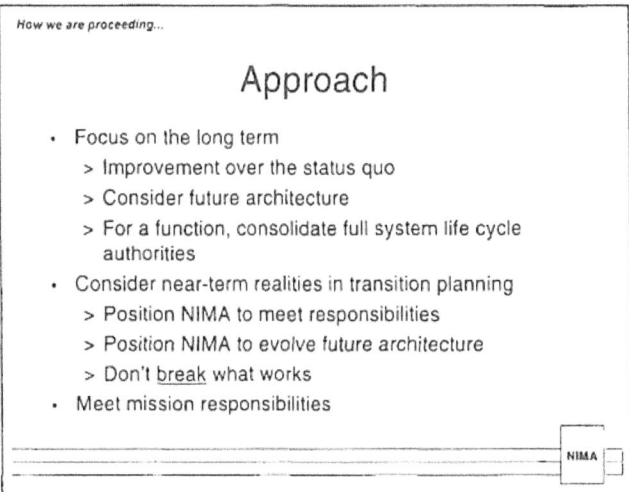

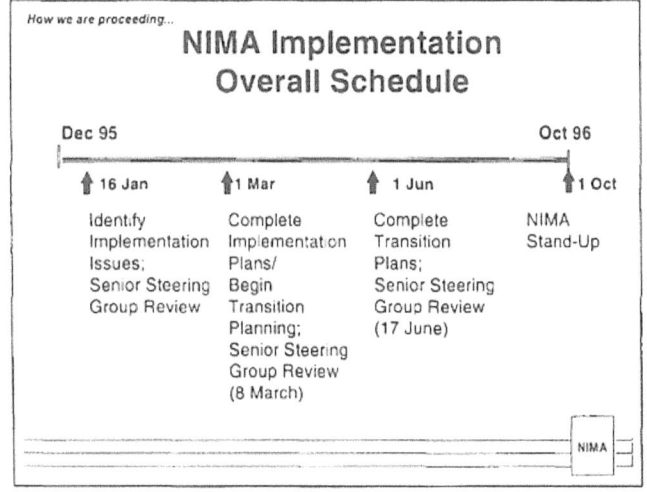

# Progress to Date

- Implementation Team stand-up on 4 December
- Located in full-service DMA facilities in Reston
- Initial activities focused on:
  - > Establishing Working Groups to identify issues and concepts of operations
  - > Congressional consultation began on 15 December
  - > Internal Communications
  - > Crafting NIMA mission and vision
- Stakeholders Off-site on 13 December
- Working Group start-up on 19 December
- Senior Steering Group Review on 16 January
- Military Intelligence Board on 24 January

NIMA

---

# NIMA Mission

NIMA provides timely, relevant, and accurate imagery intelligence and geospatial information products and services in support of national security objectives

NIMA

# NIMA Responsibilities

- Understand customer needs
- Perform imagery analysis and geospatial information production
- Manage and task national collection operations
- Ensure primary and secondary dissemination
- Manage archives of original national and tactical imagery
- Develop and enforce technical standards and configuration control

NIMA

# NIMA Responsibilities (cont'd)

- Define and recommend policies (e.g., releaseability)
- Establish end-to-end architecture
- Develop investment plan
- Conduct or sponsor research and development
- Provide full system life cycle support
- Establish career programs, training standards, and curricula for imagery analysts and cartographers

NIMA

## Working Groups

- Human Resources (Chair - CIA)
- Program & Budget (Chair - DIA)
- Responsibilities and Boundary Issues (Chair - CIO)
- Legal Issues - Directives, Statutes, Authorities (Chair - DMA)
- Contracting Activities (Chair - )
- Organizational Issues and Alternatives (Chair - DMA)
- Infrastructure (Chair - CIO)
- Strategic Planning (Chair - NPIC)

NIMA

## Working Group Purpose

- Identify key issues for resolution prior to NIMA implementation
- Prepare concepts of operations to guide future Transition Teams
- Learn from experience of broad range of individuals with a stake in NIMA's success
- Initiate the process of buy-in to NIMA concepts

NIMA

## Responsibilities and Boundary Issues Working Group

- Description:
  - Determine and document the NIMA responsibilities for all aspects of imagery intelligence and geospatial information
  - Describe the interfaces between NIMA and NRO, DARO and DDPO concerning collection, processing, exploitation and dissemination
  - Describe the interface between: NIMA and CIA; NIMA and DIA
- Deliverables and Schedule
  - Jan 96:    Definition of NIMA responsibilities and completed interface descriptions; recommendations on any unresolved issues; briefing to Implementation Team
  - Feb 96:    Recommendation refinements; complete scheduled activity

NIMA

## Human Resources Working Group

- Description:
  - Baseline existing human resources practices
  - Identify human resources authorities including competitive service, title authorities, unions and hiring authorities
  - Identify human resources issues and develop a concept of operations for HR services
- Deliverables and schedule:
  - Jan 96:    Define issues and recommendations; briefing to Implementation Team
  - Feb 96:    Concept of Operations; HR Structure (Career service, training, career progression, etc.); briefing to Implementation Team

NIMA

## Contracting Activities Working Group

- **Description:**
  - Baseline existing, soon-to-be awarded and planned contracts
  - Describe contracting authorities, processes and capabilities of incoming NIMA organizations
  - Define issues and propose alternatives for transition to a NIMA contracting activity
- **Deliverables and schedule:**
  - Catalog ongoing/planned contracts by organization, type, duration, related issues; describe incoming and supporting organizations capabilities
  - Feb 96:    Initial brief to Implementation Team on NIMA required contracting capabilities, alternatives and issues
  - Mar 96:    Contracting Activities CONOPs

NIMA

## Organizational Issues
## and Alternatives Working Group

- **Description:**
  - Baseline:
    - Existing customers, products and services (external and internal)
    - Research, development, acquisition and O&M activities
    - International activities
    - Information services and
    - Management practices
  - Describe what we do well, what we don't do well, and what's not being done.
  - Define NIMA core business processes
  - Identify customer needs and assure delivery of the right products and services
  - Define NIMA missions and functions; establish top-level NIMA Concept of Operation; define alternative organizational structures
- **Deliverable and schedule**
  - Feb 96:    Organizational activity baseline; NIMA missions and functions; NIMA CONOPs
  - Feb 96:    NIMA organizational framework and resource crosswalk

NIMA

## Infrastructure Working Group

- Description:
  - Baseline existing practices and present planned improvements in:
    - Facilities/installation management
    - Financial management, and
    - All aspects of security
  - Identify best practices in each area
  - Recommend alternative concepts of operation for the delivery of effective consolidated support services
- Deliverables and schedule:
  - Feb 96:    Baseline description of each service area; identification of best practices
  - Feb 96:    Alternative CONOPs each service area

NIMA

## Strategic Planning Working Group

- Description:
  - Baseline existing efforts at strategic planning
  - Identify top-level prioritization and allocation of resources
  - Catalogue assessments of product quality and customer satisfaction
  - Describe application of metrics to assess performance
  - Identify best practices in each area and recommend alternative concepts of operation for implementing an effective process for strategic planning and performance assessment
- Deliverables and schedule:
  - Feb 96:    Description of existing processes and identification of best practices; briefing to Implementation Team
  - Feb 96:    Alternative concepts of operation for robust and effective processes for strategic planning, resource allocation, and performance assessment; process recommendations for the Transition Plan

NIMA

## Working Group Process

- Kickoff Week (18-22 December):
    - > Receive overview and charter from Implementation Team Director
    - > Take opportunity to organize team through such things as . . .
        - » Creation of work plan based on schedules and deliverables
        - » Development of "rules of engagement" and decision processes
        - » Clarification of guidance
    - > Identify key issues requiring resolution by during Implementation . . . categorize into two groups:
        - » Issues requiring early resolution - to be presented 10 January in anticipation of 15 January Steering Group meeting
        - » Issues that can be resolved between 15 January and 1 March
    - > Schedule briefing from "summer study" counterpart group chairperson . . .for delivery as soon as feasible for team and briefer

NIMA

## Working Group Process

- Jan - March:
    - > Create sub-groups as needed to facilitate task accomplishment . . . draw in other resources when necessary
    - > Keep Implementation Team advised of progress, issues, concerns
        - » Weekly meetings
        - » Informal communications with Sponsor
    - > Stay apprised of other teams' progress to assure integration of total effort

NIMA

# APPENDIX I

## NIMA DECISION PROCESS
## 6 FEB 96 BRIEFING CHART

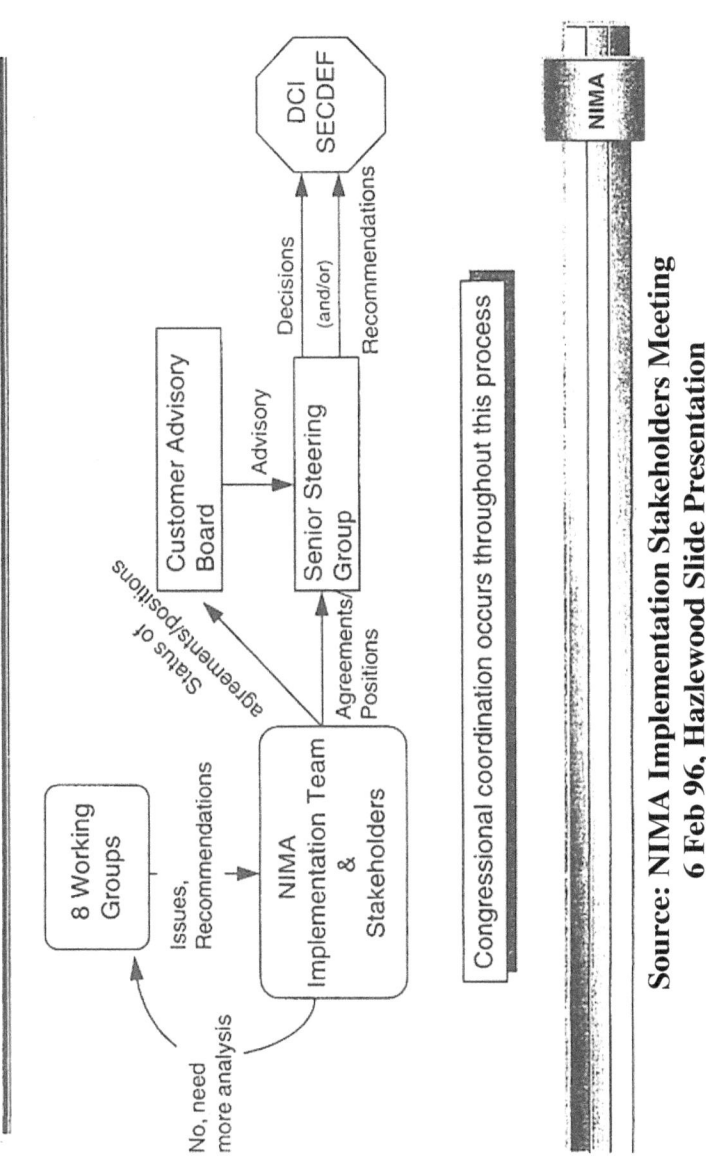

**Source: NIMA Implementation Stakeholders Meeting**
**6 Feb 96, Hazlewood Slide Presentation**

# APPENDIX J

## IMAGERY FUNCTIONAL MANAGEMENT
## 6 FEB BRIEFING CHART

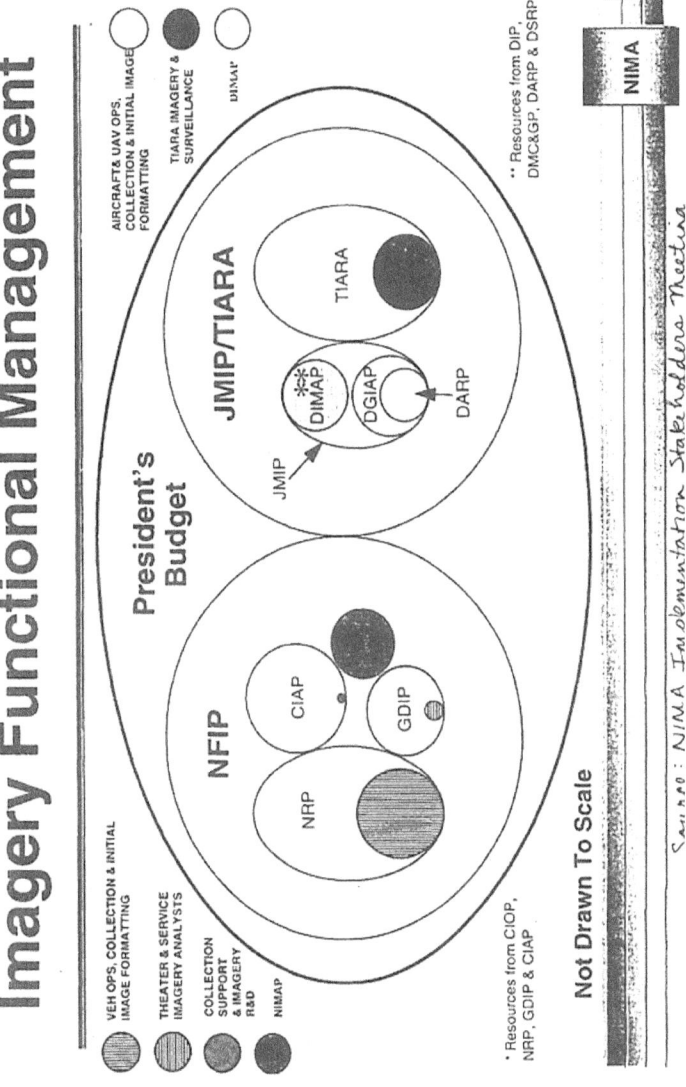

**Source: NIMA Implementation Stakeholders Meeting
6 Feb 96, Hazlewood Slide Presentation**

# APPENDIX K

## NIMA—WHAT'S INCLUDED CHART

**Source: Status Report on Implementation Planning for NIMA presented to NRO/IMINT Employmees 10 April 96, Hazlewood Slide Presentation**

*Responsibilities & Boundaries*

# What Is Included (1)

- Systems to perform imagery tasking, processing after image formation, exploitation, or dissemination
  - Requirements Management System (RMS)
  - Enhanced Processing Segment (EPS)
  - Custom Product Activity (CPA)
  - Custom Product Network (CPN)
  - Defense Dissemination System (DDS) Receive Elements (REs)
  - Accelerated Architecture Acquisition Initiative ($A^3I$)
  - Digital Production System (DPS)
  - Imagery Data Exploitation System (IDEX)
  - AIRES Life Extension (ALE)
  - NPIC Data System (NDS)
  - Common Imagery Ground Surface System (CIG/SS)
  - Imagery Exploitation Support System (IESS)
  - DIA Photo Lab (partial)

NIMA

4/10/96    8 03 AM

# What Is Included (2)

- **R&D for exploitation and dissemination, including:**
  - Advanced R&D from DARO and the NRO
  - Prototype Development Facility (partial)
  - National Imagery Display and National Media Laboratories
- **CIO authorities on imagery policy**
- **NIMA assumes responsibility on imagery policy for:**
  - Second Party programs and management of TK billets
  - Third Party programs
  - Classification, release, and disclosure for all non-national airborne missions
  - Legal review of domestic imaging requests **(pending decision)**
- **Delegated disclosure authority for NTM remains at CIA**

NIMA

v2

4/10/96   8:03 AM

# What Is Included (3)

- Personnel from CIO, USAF (including DDPO and NRO), DIA (including imagery elements) and DMA

- Operational control of all NPIC and selected individuals from OD&E and CRES

- Defense Counter Drug Program

- Timing of programmatic transitions to be worked in the next phase

NIMA

4/10/96    8:03 AM

79

*Responsibilities & Boundaries*

# What Is Excluded (1)

- Collection platforms, both satellite and airbreather
- On-board or ground processing through initial image formation
- Imagery intelligence and geospatial information resources in TIARA
- GDIP personnel resources in the Services and Commands
  - Imagery analysts
  - DDS maintenance personnel at the Unified Commands
- Acquisition and maintenance of site-specific capabilities

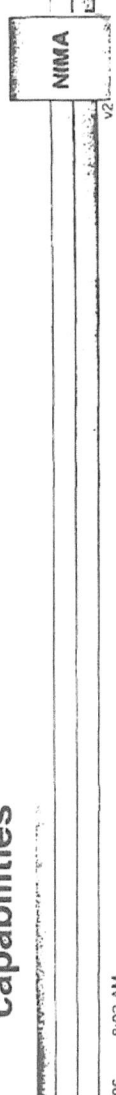

NIMA

v2

4/10/96    8:03 AM

# What Is Excluded (2)

- **Positions and associated salaries and benefits remain in the CIA Program**

  - All NPIC personnel and selected others (OD&E and CRES) are OPCON to NIMA

  - D/NIMA assigns them within NIMA

  - D/NIMA selects NIMA's managers, including those who supervise CIA personnel

    - Products created will be identified as NIMA's

- **SECDEF and DCI will review these arrangements in two years**

NIMA

V2

82

# APPENDIX M

# DoD DIRECTIVE 5105.60
# 11 OCT 96, ESTABLISHING NIMA

 Department of Defense
# DIRECTIVE

NUMBER 5105.60
October 11, 1996

DA&M

SUBJECT: National Imagery and Mapping Agency (NIMA)

References: (a) Title 10, United States Code
     (b) Title 50, United States Code
     (c) Executive Order 12333, "United States Intelligence Activities,"
       December 4, 1981
     (d) National Imagery and Mapping Agency Act of 1996
     (e) through (o), see enclosure 1

## 1. PURPOSE

This Directive:

1.1. Establishes the NIMA within the Department of Defense consistent with the authorities and duties of the Secretary of Defense and the Director of Central Intelligence (DCI) under references (a), (b), (c), and (d).

1.2. Prescribes the NIMA's mission, organization, responsibilities, functions, relationships, and authorities, pursuant to the authority vested in the Secretary of Defense by Section 113 and Chapters 8 and 22 of reference (a), and in accordance with references (a), (b), and (d).

1.3. Replaces DoD Directives 5105.40 and 5105.56 (references (e) and (f)).

## 2. APPLICABILITY

This Directive applies to the Office of the Secretary of Defense, the Military Departments, the Chairman of the Joint Chiefs of Staff, the Combatant Commands, the Office of the Inspector General of the Department of Defense, the Defense Agencies, and the DoD Field Activities (hereafter referred to collectively as "the DoD Components") and other Federal Departments and Agencies on matters related to the statutory NIMA mission.

## 3. DEFINITIONS

Terms used in this Directive are defined in enclosure 2.

## 4. MISSION

The NIMA shall provide timely, relevant, and accurate imagery, imagery intelligence, and geospatial information in support of the national security objectives of the United States.

## 5. ORGANIZATION AND MANAGEMENT

The NIMA is hereby established as a Defense Agency of the Department of Defense under the authority, direction, and control of the Secretary of Defense, and is designated as a Combat Support Agency pursuant to 10 U.S.C. 193 (reference (a)). The NIMA is an agency within the Intelligence Community in accordance with 50 U.S.C. 401a(4)(E) (reference (b)) and E.O. 12333 (reference (c)). The Assistant Secretary of Defense for Command, Control, Communications, and Intelligence (ASD(C3I)) exercises overall supervision over the NIMA pursuant to Section 192 of reference (a); however, all substantive intelligence produced by the NIMA shall be submitted directly to the Secretary and Deputy Secretary of Defense and, as appropriate, to the Chairman of the Joint Chiefs of Staff and the DCI. The NIMA shall consist of a Director, and such subordinate organizational elements as the Director establishes within the resources made available. The Director, if a military officer, shall carry the grade of lieutenant general, or, in the case of the Navy, vice admiral.

## 6. RESPONSIBILITIES AND FUNCTIONS

The Director, NIMA, advises the Secretary and Deputy Secretary of Defense, the ASD(C3I), the Chairman of the Joint Chiefs of Staff, the Combatant Commanders, and, for national intelligence purposes, the DCI and other Federal Government officials, on imagery, imagery intelligence, and geospatial information; and supports the imagery, imagery intelligence, and geospatial requirements of the Departments and Agencies of the Federal Government, to the extent provided by law. In the exercise of these responsibilities, the Director, NIMA, shall:

6.1. Organize, direct, and manage the NIMA and all assigned resources.

6.2. Provide responsive imagery, imagery intelligence and geospatial information products, support, services, and information (to include the coordination of imagery collection requirements, national tasking, processing, exploitation, and dissemination) to the DoD Components, and, for national intelligence purposes, to the DCI, the non-DoD members of the Intelligence Community, the National Security Council, and other Federal Government Departments and Agencies.

6.3. Manage imagery and geospatial analysis and production.

6.4. Manage the tasking of and task national collection operations in accordance with Section 442 of reference (a), Section 403-5(b)(2) of reference (b), and E.O. 12333 (reference (c)), and consistent with the DCI's collection tasking authority under Section 441(c) of reference (a), Section 402 et seq. of reference (b), reference (c), and DoD Directive S-3325.2 (reference (g)), as follows:

6.4.1. Developing and consolidating geospatial information requirements and national imagery collection requirements.

6.4.2. Supporting the imagery requirements of the Department of State and other non-DoD Agencies, in accordance with the requirements and priorities established by the DCI.

6.4.3. Tasking DoD imagery collection elements to meet national intelligence requirements and priorities, as established by the DCI, except as noted in paragraph 6.6., below.

6.4.4. Advising DoD imagery collection elements on the collection of imagery to meet non-national intelligence requirements.

6.5. Establish and/or consolidate DoD geospatial information data collection requirements and collecting or tasking other DoD Components to collect and provide necessary data, except as noted in paragraph 6.6., below.

6.6. Provide advisory tasking for theater and tactical assets, including advising imagery collection elements on collection of imagery to meet national intelligence requirements when the collection elements are both assigned to or under the operational control of the Secretary of a Military Department or the Commander of a Combatant Command, and not allocated by the Secretary of Defense to meet national intelligence requirements.

6.7. Disseminate or ensure the dissemination of imagery, imagery intelligence, and geospatial information by the most efficient and expeditious means consistent with DoD and DCI security requirements.

6.8. Serve as the Program Manager for the National Imagery and Mapping Program, a program within the National Foreign Intelligence Program (NFIP), for activities within the NIMA, and as Program Manager for the Defense Imagery and Mapping Program within the DoD Joint Military Intelligence Program (JMIP).

6.9. Serve as the Functional Manager for imagery, imagery intelligence, and geospatial investment activities which include RDT&E and procurement initiatives within the NFIP, JMIP, and the Tactical Intelligence and Related Activities (TIARA) aggregate.

6.10. Develop and make recommendations on national and non-national policy for imagery, imagery intelligence, and geospatial information, including as it relates to international matters, for the approval of appropriate Federal Government officials.

6.11. Prescribe and mandate standards and end-to-end technical architectures related to imagery, imagery intelligence, and geospatial information for the DoD Components and for the non-DoD elements of the Intelligence Community, in accordance with Section 442 of reference (a), and Sections 402 et seq. and 403-5(b) of reference (b), to include:

6.11.1. Standards for end-to-end architectures related to imagery, imagery intelligence, and geospatial information.

6.11.2. Standards for geospatial information products produced within DoD in accordance with DoD 4120.3-M (reference (h)).

6.11.3. Standards for career programs for imagery analysts, cartographers, and related fields.

6.11.4. Standards for training, programs and courses for advanced imagery analysts, cartographers, personnel performing imagery tasking, geospatial information collection, and imagery, imagery intelligence, and geospatial information processing, exploitation, and dissemination functions, imagery-related functional management, and related fields.

6.11.5. Technical guidance and direction to all the DoD Components and the non-DoD members of the Intelligence Community regarding standardization and interoperability of systems requiring geospatial information or imagery support.

6.11.6. Technical guidance and direction to all the DoD Components and the non-DoD members of the Intelligence Community regarding standardization and interoperability of systems for exploitation and dissemination of imagery and imagery intelligence products and geospatial information.

6.12. Establish system and end-to-end architectures related to imagery, imagery intelligence, and geospatial information, in compliance with National and Defense Information Infrastructure guidance and standards in accordance with 10 U.S.C. 442 (reference (a)) and 50 U.S.C. 402 et seq. (reference (b)), by:

6.12.1. Performing or directing the research, design, development, deployment operation and maintenance of systems related to the processing, dissemination, and archiving of imagery (including tasking, processing, exploitation, and dissemination), imagery intelligence, and geospatial information.

6.12.2. Transferring or otherwise providing such systems to the DoD Components and to other Federal Government Agencies, as appropriate.

6.12.3. Developing and fielding systems of common concern related to imagery intelligence and geospatial information.

6.13. Evaluate the performance of imagery, imagery intelligence, and geospatial information components of the Department of Defense in meeting national and military intelligence requirements. To the extent authorized by the DCI, evaluate the performance of the non-DoD Departments or Agencies of the Intelligence Community having imagery or geospatial information tasking, collection, processing, exploitation, and dissemination functions, in meeting national and non-national intelligence requirements. Report evaluation results annually to the Secretary of Defense, the Chairman of the Joint Chiefs of Staff, and the DCI. Define and recommend cooperative production and dissemination arrangements for the performance of imagery, imagery intelligence, and geospatial information components of the Department of Defense and the Intelligence Community to support wartime and emergency operations.

6.14. Coordinate efforts of the DoD Components to provide their Tactical Impact Statements to the Congress on the ability of proposed national systems to satisfy tactical requirements.

6.15. Review and respond to the imagery, imagery intelligence, and geospatial information requirements and priorities for military operations, in support of the Chairman of the Joint Chiefs of Staff and the Combatant Commanders.

6.16. Develop and submit to the Secretary of Defense a consolidated statement of the geospatial information production requirements and priorities in accordance with the National Military Strategy and the national security objectives of the United States.

6.17. Review and validate the national reconnaissance imagery and imagery intelligence requirements and priorities for national customers, and develop and submit to the DCI a consolidated statement of these imagery and imagery intelligence requirements and priorities in accordance with policies and procedures established by the DCI.

6.18. Manage the national archive of national and appropriate tactical imagery, imagery products, and geospatial information.

6.19. Exercise imagery and geospatial information systems for responsiveness and support to military forces in preparation for wartime and emergency operations.

6.20. In accordance with the DoD Plan for Peacetime Use of Reserve Component Intelligence Elements, dated December 21, 1994, identify imagery, and imagery intelligence tasks, products, support services, and information requirements that can appropriately be satisfied from within the Military Services' Reserve Forces. In coordination with the Defense Intelligence Agency and the Military Services, establish the capability to conduct mission tasking and mission management of Reserve Forces engaged in or capable of being engaged in these activities.

6.21. Develop policies and provide DoD participation in national and international imagery, imagery intelligence, and geospatial information activities, in coordination with appropriate DoD officials for geospatial information activities and with the DCI for imagery activities and activities which involve an intelligence or security service of a foreign country. Represent the Department of Defense in national and international geospatial information standardization activities. Execute DoD responsibilities under interagency and international geospatial information agreements.

6.22.  Protect intelligence sources and methods from unauthorized disclosure pursuant to guidance received from the DCI in accordance with the National Security Act of 1947 (50 U.S.C., reference (b)), E.O. 12333 (reference (c)), PDD NSTC-8 (reference(i)), E.O. 12951 (reference (j)), and E.O. 12958 (reference (k)).

6.23.  Advise the Secretary of Defense and the DCI on future needs for imagery, imagery intelligence, and geospatial information capabilities and systems, as appropriate.

6.24.  Provide staff advice and assistance on imagery, imagery intelligence, and geospatial information related matters to the DoD Components and other Federal Government Departments and Agencies, as appropriate.

6.25.  Serve as the sole DoD action agency for all purchases of commercial and foreign government-owned imagery-related remote sensing data by the DoD Components.  Serve as the primary action agency for such purchases by any other Federal Department or Agency, on request.

6.26.  Advise the Defense Acquisition Board, the Defense Science Board, the Joint Space Management Board, and other DoD boards on imagery, imagery intelligence, and geospatial information issues, as appropriate.

6.27.  Identify and analyze the industrial base, as appropriate, to meet essential customer imagery requirements and to ensure industrial base impacts on NIMA functions are considered.  Assess the applicability of evolving commercial capabilities to meet imagery and geospatial information needs of the Department of Defense and the Intelligence Community.

6.28.  Establish and maintain a NIMA Joint Manpower Program that will be reviewed annually by the Chairman of the Joint Chiefs of Staff.

6.29.  Serve as the DoD Modeling and Simulation Management Executive Agent for Terrain, managing and overseeing all aspects of DoD modeling and simulation related to the authoritative representation of terrain, including both data and the dynamic process models describing related natural and man-made effects, in accordance with DoD 5000.59-P (reference (l)).

6.30.  Protect the security of NIMA installations, activities, property, information, and employees by all appropriate means in accordance with statute and DoD regulations.

6.31. Consistent with DoD and DCI policies, promulgate procedures and instructions for imagery, imagery intelligence, and geospatial information and related matters to the Department of Defense, as necessary, including publication of handbooks for the exploitation, analysis, dissemination and release of imagery, imagery-derived products, and geospatial information.

6.32. Establish a Chief Information Officer, with responsibilities and functions as provided in Division E of Pub.L. 104-106 (1996) (reference (m)).

6.33. Perform such other functions as the Secretary of Defense may direct.

## 7. RELATIONSHIPS

7.1. In performing assigned functions, the Director, NIMA, subject to the authority, direction, and control of the Secretary of Defense and the overall supervision of the ASD(C3I), shall:

7.1.1. Be responsible to the Chairman of the Joint Chiefs of Staff for matters affecting the Chairman's responsibilities under Title 10 U.S.C. (reference (a)), especially requirements associated with the joint planning process, and for matters affecting the missions and responsibilities of the Combatant Commanders. For these purposes, the Chairman of the Joint Chiefs of Staff is authorized to communicate directly with, and task, the Director, NIMA.

7.1.2. Exchange information and advice and coordinate actions with the Heads of the other DoD Components having collateral or related functions, as appropriate.

7.1.3. Maintain liaison with Executive Branch organizations on imagery and geospatial matters, as appropriate.

7.1.4. To the extent permitted by law, use established facilities and services of the Department of Defense or other Federal Government Departments or Agencies, whenever practicable, to avoid duplication and achieve an appropriate balance of modernization, efficiency, and economy of operations. Special emphasis should be placed on maximizing use of existing personnel, facilities, and services of the DoD Intelligence Components, and, to the extent authorized by the DCI, the Central Intelligence Agency.

7.2. The Heads of the DoD Components shall:

7.2.1. Provide assistance and support to the Director, NIMA, in their respective fields of responsibility and within available resources, as may be necessary to carry out functions assigned to the NIMA.

7.2.2. Ensure compliance with taskings issued by the Director, NIMA, pursuant to this Directive.

7.2.3. Submit imagery, imagery intelligence, and geospatial collection and production requirements to the Director, NIMA, in accordance with procedures established by the Chairman of the Joint Chiefs of Staff.

7.2.4. Coordinate with the Director, NIMA, on all matters concerning the mission, capabilities, functions, and operations of the NIMA.

7.3. The Chairman of the Joint Chiefs of Staff shall review and assess the responsiveness and readiness of the NIMA to support operating forces in the event of a war or threat to national security and make any recommendations the Chairman considers appropriate, in accordance with Section 193 of 10 U.S.C. (reference (a)).

## 8. AUTHORITY

8.1. The ASD(C3I) is delegated the authority to issue Instructions to the DoD Components to implement this Directive. Instructions to the Military Departments shall be issued through the Secretaries of the Military Departments. Instructions to the Combatant Commanders shall be issued through the Chairman of the Joint Chiefs of Staff.

8.2. The Director, NIMA, is specifically delegated authority to:

8.2.1. Obtain reports, information, advice, and assistance, consistent with DoD Directive 4630.5 (reference (n)) and DoD Directive 8910.1 (reference (o)), as necessary, to carry out assigned functions.

8.2.2. Communicate directly with the heads of the DoD Components, the Intelligence Community, and other Federal Government Departments and Agencies, as necessary, to carry out assigned functions. Communications to the Combatant Commanders shall be coordinated, as appropriate, with the Chairman of the Joint

Chiefs of Staff.

8.2.3. Exercise functional oversight over the United States Imagery System (USIS) and the Geospatial Information Infrastructure (GII); such oversight shall include the requisite technical oversight authority over the tactical elements of the USIS and GII to ensure interoperability between existing and future USIS and GII systems, connectivity between national and tactical systems, and modernization of tactical systems.

8.2.4. Exercise the administrative authorities in enclosure 3.

8.3. The Director, NIMA, shall exercise the authorities and responsibilities of a Senior Official of the Intelligence Community pursuant to the National Security Act of 1947 (50 U.S.C., reference (b)), E.O. 12333 (reference (c)), and the NIMA Act of 1996 (reference (d)).

## 9. ADMINISTRATION

9.1. The Director, NIMA, shall be appointed and evaluated by the Secretary of Defense in accordance with 10 U.S.C. 201 (reference (a)).

9.2. The Military Departments shall assign military personnel to the NIMA in accordance with approved Joint Manpower Program authorizations and procedures for assignment to joint duty. The Chairman of the Joint Chiefs of Staff shall review NIMA joint staffing program requirements for those functions related to NIMA direct intelligence support to the Chairman of the Joint Chiefs of Staff, and provide appropriate recommendations to the ASD(C3I).

9.3. The NIMA shall be authorized such personnel, facilities, funds, and other resources as the Secretary of Defense deems appropriate. The NIMA may obtain personnel, administrative, and contracting support from the Central Intelligence Agency, to the extent permitted by law and approved by the Secretary of Defense and the DCI.

10. EFFECTIVE DATE

This Directive is effective on October 1, 1996.

John P. White
Deputy Secretary of Defense

Enclosures - 3
1. References
2. Definitions
3. Delegations of Authority

## E1. ENCLOSURE 1

## REFERENCES continued

(e) DoD Directive 5105.40, "Defense Mapping Agency (DMA)," December 6, 1990 (hereby canceled)

(f) DoD Directive 5105.56, "Central Imagery Office (CIO)", October 23, 1995 (hereby canceled)

(g) DoD Directive S-3325.2, "Transfer of National Intelligence Collection Tasking Authority (U)," June 18, 1987

(h) DoD 4120.3-M, "Defense Standardization Program (DSP) Policies and Procedures," July 1993, authorized by DoD 5000.2-R, March 15, 1996

(i) Presidential Decision Directive NSTC-8, "National Space Policy (U)," September 14, 1996

(j) Executive Order 12951, "Release of Imagery Acquired by Space Based National Intelligence Reconnaissance Systems," February 22, 1995

(k) Executive Order 12958, "Classified National Security Information," April 17, 1995

(l) DoD 5000.59-P, "Modeling and Simulation (M&S) Master Plan," October 1995, authorized by DoD Directive 5000.59, January 4, 1994

(m) Public Law 104-106, "National Defense Authorization Act for Fiscal Year 1996," February 10, 1996

(n) DoD Directive 4630.5, "Compatibility, Interoperability, and Integration of Command, Control, Communications, and Intelligence (C3I) Systems," November 12, 1992

(o) DoD Directive 8910.1, "Management and Control of Information Requirements," June 11, 1993

## E2. ENCLOSURE 2

## DEFINITIONS

E2.1.1.  Advisory Tasking.  The submission of national requirements for collection, as appropriate, by theater and tactical reconnaissance platforms.

E2.1.2.  Functional Management.

E2.1.2.1.  The review of and coordination on investment activities related to imagery, imagery intelligence, and geospatial information, which includes RDT&E, and procurement activities within the NFIP, JMIP, and TIARA aggregate.  Review includes imagery-related fiscal and personnel resources, Program Objective Memoranda and budget submissions to affect resource allocation decisions and assure compliance with architecture, equipment, and data and related standards and policy, in accordance with Section 105(b)(2) of the National Security Act of 1947 (50 U.S.C.) (reference (b)), as amended.

E2.1.2.2.  Provision of program planning and resource guidance to the DoD Components for the development of inputs to the Planning, Programming, and Budgeting System and to the Intelligence Community agencies for inputs to the Capabilities Programming and Budgeting System.

E2.1.3.  Geospatial Information.  Information that identifies the geographic location and characteristics of natural or constructed features and boundaries on the earth, including: statistical data; information derived from, among other things, remote sensing, mapping, and surveying technologies; and mapping, charting and geodetic data, including "geodetic products," as that term is used in Chapter 167 of 10 U.S.C. (reference (a)).

E2.1.4.  Geospatial Information Infrastructure.  The collection of technology, policies, standards, capabilities, services, and doctrine necessary to produce, maintain, disseminate, and exploit geospatial information.  This includes the links between global geospatial information and sophisticated geographic information system technologies that allow desktop import and export of geospatial data sets; that assure interactive and reliable data manipulation, update, and value adding; and that encourage dissemination through the use of electronic gateways and networks.

E2.1.5.  Imagery.  A likeness or representation of any natural or man-made feature or related object or activity and the positional data acquired at the same time the likeness or representation was acquired, including products produced by space-based national intelligence reconnaissance systems, and likenesses or representations produced by satellites, airborne platforms, unmanned aerial vehicles, or other similar means (except that such term does not include handheld or clandestine photography taken by or on behalf of human intelligence collection organizations).

E2.1.6. Imagery Intelligence. The technical, geographic, and intelligence information derived through the interpretation or analysis of imagery and collateral materials.

E2.1.7. Imagery Related or End - to - End Architectures. The means by which imagery-related information flows from the collectors and producers to the customers. The term includes guiding principles , design concepts, standards, capabilities, customer feedback, and relationships of imagery-related organizations and systems.

E2.1.8. Intelligence Community. Has the same meaning as in Executive Order 12333 (reference (c)) and Section 3 of the National Security Act of 1947 (50 U.S.C.) (reference (b)), as amended.

E2.1.9. Defense Imagery and Mapping Program (DIMP). Imagery, imagery intelligence, and geospatial fiscal and personnel resources program, for which the Director, NIMA is Program Manager, of the DoD Joint Military Intelligence Program (JMIP). (Formerly the Defense Imagery Program and the Defense Mapping, Charting, and Geodesy Program in the JMIP.)

E2.1.10. Mapping, Charting, and Geodetic Data. Comprises the collection, transformation, generation, dissemination, and storing of geodetic, geomagnetic, gravimetric, aeronautical, topographic, hydrographic, cultural, and toponymic data. These data may be presented in the form of topographic, planimetric, relief, or thematic maps and graphics; nautical and aeronautical charts and publications; and in simulated, photographic, digital, or computerized formats. Has the same meaning as mapping, charting and geodesy.

E2.1.11. National Imagery and Mapping Program (NIMP). Imagery, imagery intelligence, and geospatial fiscal and personnel resources program, within the National Foreign Intelligence Program, for which the Director, NIMA, is Program Manager.

E2.1.12. United States Imagery System (USIS). All of the imagery capabilities of the United States Government (USG) as well as all the imagery, imagery data, and imagery-derived products produced by or for the USG.  It includes the functional areas of requirements and needs management, collection, processing, exploitation, production, and dissemination.

E3. ENCLOSURE 3

DELEGATIONS OF AUTHORITY

E3.1.1. Pursuant to the authority vested in the Secretary of Defense, and subject to the authority, direction, and control of the Secretary of Defense, and in accordance with DoD policies, Directives, and Instructions, the Director, NIMA, or, in the absence of the Director, the person acting for the Director, is hereby delegated authority as required in the administration and operation of the NIMA to:

E3.1.1.1. Exercise the authority vested in the Secretary of Defense by 5 U.S.C. 301, 302(b), 3101 and 5107, and Chapter 83 of 10 U.S.C., as amended, on the employment, direction, and general administration of NIMA civilian personnel.

E3.1.1.2. Fix rates of pay for wage-rate employees exempted from the Classification Act of 1949 by 5 U.S.C. 5102 on the basis of rates established under the Coordinated Federal Wage System. In fixing such rates, the Director, NIMA, shall follow the wage schedule established by the DoD Wage Fixing Authority.

E3.1.1.3. Administer oaths of office to those entering the Executive Branch of the Federal Government or any other oath required by law in connection with employment therein, in accordance with 5 U.S.C. 2903, and designate in writing, as may be necessary, officers and employees of the NIMA to perform this function.

E3.1.1.4. Maintain an official seal and attest to the authenticity of official NIMA records under that seal.

E3.1.1.5. Establish a NIMA Incentive Awards Board, and pay cash awards to, and incur necessary expenses for, the honorary recognition of civilian employees of the Government whose suggestions, inventions, superior accomplishments, or other personal efforts, including special acts or services, benefit or affect the NIMA, in accordance with 5 U.S.C. 4503, Office of Personnel Management (OPM) regulations, and DoD Directive 5120.15, "Authority for Approval of Cash Honorary Awards for DoD Personnel," August 13, 1985.

E3.1.1.6. Act as agent for the collection and payment of employment taxes imposed by appropriate statutes.

E3.1.1.7. Establish advisory committees and employ temporary or intermittent experts or consultants, as approved by the Secretary of Defense, for the performance of NIMA functions consistent with 10 U.S.C. 173, 5 U.S.C. 3109(b), and DoD Directive 5105.4, "Department of Defense Federal Advisory Committee Management Program," September 5, 1989.

E3.1.1.8. In accordance with Executive Orders 10450, 12333, 12958, 12968, and DoD Directive 5200.2, "Department of Defense Personnel Security Program," May 6, 1992, as appropriate:

E3.1.1.8.1. Designate any position in the NIMA as a "sensitive" position.

E3.1.1.8.2. Authorize, in the case of an emergency, the appointment of a person to a sensitive position in the NIMA for a limited period of time and for whom a full field investigation or other appropriate investigation, including the National Agency Check, has not been completed.

E3.1.1.8.3. Initiate personnel security investigations and, if necessary in the interest of national security, suspend a security clearance for personnel assigned, detailed to, or employed by the NIMA. Any action under this paragraph shall be taken in accordance with procedures prescribed in DoD 5200.2-R, "Department of Defense Personnel Security Program," January 1987.

E3.1.1.9. Authorize and approve:

E3.1.1.9.1. Temporary duty travel for military personnel assigned or detailed to the NIMA in accordance with Joint Federal Travel Regulations, Volume I, "Uniformed Service Members."

E3.1.1.9.2. Travel for NIMA civilian employees in accordance with Joint Travel Regulations, Volume 2, "DoD Civilian Personnel."

E3.1.1.9.3. Invitational travel to non-DoD personnel whose consultative, advisory, or other highly specialized technical services are required in a capacity that is directly related to, or in connection with, NIMA activities, in accordance with 5 U.S.C. 5703 and Joint Travel Regulations, Volume 2, "DoD Civilian Personnel."

E3.1.1.9.4. Overtime work for NIMA civilian employees in accordance with 5 U.S.C. Chapter 55, Subchapter V, and applicable OPM regulations.

E3.1.1.10. Approve the expenditure of funds available for travel by military personnel assigned or detailed to the NIMA for expenses incident to attendance at meetings of technical, scientific, professional, or other similar organizations in such instances when the approval of the Secretary of Defense, or designee, is required by 37 U.S.C. 412, and 5 U.S.C. 4110 and 4111.

E3.1.1.11. Develop, establish, and maintain an active and continuing Records Management Program, pursuant to 44 U.S.C. 3102 and DoD Directive 5015.2, "Records Management Program," March 22, 1991.

E3.1.1.12. Authorize the publication of advertisements, notices, or proposals in newspapers, magazines, or other public periodicals, as required for the effective administration and operation of the NIMA, consistent with 44 U.S.C. 3702.

E3.1.1.13. Establish and maintain, for the functions assigned, an appropriate publications system for the promulgation of common supply and service regulations, instructions, and reference documents, and changes thereto, pursuant to the policies and procedures described in DoD 5025.1-M, "DoD Directives System Procedures," August 1994.

E3.1.1.14. Enter into support and service agreements with the Military Departments, other DoD Components, or other Federal Government Agencies, as required, for the effective performance of NIMA responsibilities and functions.

E3.1.1.15. Enter into and administer contracts, directly or through a Military Department, a DoD contract administration services component, or other Federal Agency, as appropriate, for supplies, equipment, and services required to accomplish the mission of the NIMA. To the extent that any law or Executive order specifically limits the exercise of such authority to persons at the Secretarial level of a Military Department, such authority shall be exercised by the appropriate Under Secretary or Assistant Secretary of Defense.

E3.1.1.16. Exercise the authority delegated to the Secretary of Defense by the Administrator of the General Services Administration on the disposal of surplus personal property.

E3.1.1.17. Promulgate the necessary security regulations for the protection of property and places under the jurisdiction of the Director, NIMA, pursuant to DoD Directive 5200.8, "Security of DoD Installations and Resources," April 25, 1991.

E3.1.1.18. Establish and maintain appropriate property accounts for NIMA and appoint Boards of Survey, approve reports of survey, relieve personal liability, and drop accountability for NIMA property contained in the authorized property accounts that has been lost, damaged, stolen, destroyed, or otherwise rendered unserviceable, in

ENCLOSURE 3

accordance with applicable laws and regulations.

E3.1.1.19. Sell maps, charts, and other publications to the public at prices and under regulations that may be prescribed by the Secretary of Defense, under 10 U.S.C. 453.

E3.1.1.20. Execute responsibilities of 10 U.S.C. 454 relating to international agreements.

E3.1.1.21. Withhold from sale and public disclosure geospatial information, including maps, charts, and other geodetic products, restricted by international agreement, revealing sensitive sources and methods used to obtain source material for production of the geospatial information, or jeopardize or interfere with ongoing military or intelligence operations or reveal military operational or contingency plans, pursuant to 10 U.S.C. 455.

E3.1.1.22. Lease non-excess property under the control of the NIMA, under terms that will promote the national defense or that will be in the public interest, under 10 U.S.C. 2667.

E3.1.1.23. Administer DoD and DCI security policies and programs within the NIMA.

E3.1.1.24. Serve as the Designated Approving Authority for NIMA automated information systems and networks for less than Acquisition Category (ACAT) 1A programs, or serve as the milestone decision authority (MDA) for ACAT 1A programs when delegated by the ASD(C3I). The Director, NIMA, shall exercise delegated MDA in accordance with DoD Directive 5000.1, "Defense Acquisition," March 15, 1996 and DoD 5000.2-R, "Mandatory Procedures for Major Defense Acquisition Programs and Major Automated Information System Acquisition Programs," March 1996.

E3.1.1.25 The Director, NIMA, may redelegate these authorities, as appropriate, and in writing, except as otherwise provided by law or regulation.

E3.1.1.26 These delegations of authority are effective immediately.

# BIBLIOGRAPHY

Basso, Sharon. Director of Communications and Congressional Liaison, NIMA Implementation Team. Interview by the author by email, 1 January 2001.

Battaglia, Charlie. Staff Director, Senate Select Committee on Intelligence in 1996. Interview by the author, 24 August 2000.

Best, Richard A. Jr. "Intelligence Reorganization in the 104th Congress: Prospects for A More Corporate Community," *CRS Report for Congress* no. 96-681F. Washington DC: CRS, 13 Sep 96.

Birnbaum, Jeffrey and Alan S. Murray. *Showdown at Gucci Gulch*. NY: Vintage Books, 1987.

Broadhurst, David. Director, NIMA College. Interview by the author, 27 November 2000.

Brown, Harold; Rudman, Warren and Les Aspin. *Preparing for the 21st Century: An Appraisal of U.S. Intelligence*. Washington, DC: Commission on the Roles and Capabilities of the U.S. Intelligence Community, 1 March 1996.

"Creating the National Imagery and Mapping Agency (U): A Studies Roundtable," in *Studies in Intelligence*, 42, 1 (1998): 39-49.

Davidson, Roger and Walter Oleszek. *Congress and Its Members*. Washington, DC: CQ Press, 2000.

"DCI Plans a National Imagery Agency," *DIA Communique* 7, no. 8 (Aug 1995): 1.

Duncan, Philip D. and Christine Lawrence. *Politics in America 1996: the 104th Congress*. Washington, DC: Congressional Quarterly, 1995.

Elkins, Dan. *An Intelligence Resource Manager's Guide*. Washington, DC: DIA, 1997.

Fialka, John. "Congress Set to Approve Big Review of Costly U.S. Intelligence Community," *Wall Street Journal*, 26 Sep 1994, 6.

Gates, Robert. *From the Shadows*. NY: Simon and Schuster, 1996.

_____. "Statement on Change in the IC. U.S. Congress, Joint Committee Hearings, 1 April 1992." *American Intelligence Journal* (Winter/Spring 1992): 10.

Hazlewood, Leo. Deputy Director, NIMA Implementation Team. Interview by the author, 6 October 2000.

Independent Commission on the National Imagery and Mapping Agency. *Report of the Independent Commission on the National Imagery and Mapping Agency*. Washington D.C.: GPO, 2001. URL: <*http://www.nimacommission.com*>. Accessed 21 Jan 01.

Johnson, Loch. *A Season of Inquiry: The Senate Intelligence Investigation*. Lexington: University of Kentucky Press, 1985.

Kerrey, Senator Robert (D-NE). *Congressional Record* (26 June 1996), vol. 142, no. 96.

King, David. *Turf Wars: How Congressional Committees Claim Jurisdiction*. Chicago: University of Chicago Press, 1997.

Lowenthal, Mark. Staff Director, House Permanent Senate Committee on Intelligence in 1996. Interview with author, 24 August 2000.

*Memorandum of Agreement, 26 April 1996, between the SASC and SSCI, Relating to the JMIP and TIARA.*

"NIMA Decision Brief," October 1995 Joint Chiefs of Staff "Tank" Presentation.

Obloy, Edward. General Counsel, NIMA Implementation Team. Interview by the author, 4 October 2000.

Oleszek, Walter. *Congressional Procedures and the Policy Process.* Washington, DC: CQ Press, 1989.

Pincus, Walter. "Intelligence Battleground: Reform Bill." *Washington Post*, 30 May 1996, A29.

Redman, Eric. *Dance of Legislation.* NY: Simon and Schuster, 1973.

Smist, Frank J. Jr. *Congress Oversees the U.S. Intelligence Community: 1947–1994.* Knoxville: University of Tennessee, 1994.

Snider, L. Britt. *Sharing Secrets with Lawmakers.* Washington, DC: Center for the Study of Intelligence, 1997.

A source, HPSCI Professional Staffer in 2000, who wishes to remain anonymous. Interview by the author, 5 May 2000.

A source, SASC Professional Staffer in 1996, who wishes to remain anonymous. Interview by the author, 26 Sep 2000.

A source, SSCI Professional Staffer in 1996, who wishes to remain anonymous. Interview by the author, 14 July 2000.

U.S. Congress, House, Permanent Senate Committee on Intelligence. *IC-21: Intelligence Community in the 21st Century.* Washington, DC: Government Printing Office, 1996.

U.S. Congress, House, *Rules of the 106th Congress.* Washington, DC: Government Printing Office, 1998.

U.S. Congress, Senate, *Resolution 400*, 94th Congress, 2d Session. Washington, DC: Government Printing Office, 1976.

U.S. Congress, Senate, Armed Services Committee, *Report 104-277*, 104th Congress, 2d Session. Washington, DC: Government Printing Office, 1996.

U.S. Congress, Senate, Select Committee on Intelligence, *Confirmation Hearings of John Deutch*, 94th Congress, 2nd sess., 26 April 1995.

U.S. Congress, Senate, Select Intelligence Committee, *Report 104-278*, 104th Congress, 2d Session. Washington, DC: Government Printing Office, 1996.

Waller, Douglas. "Undesignated Director." *Time*, 20 March 1995, 37.

Wise, David. "I Spy a Makeover," *Washington Post*, 30 May 1996, A 29.

For further information about Congress and its members, or to access the contents of legislation referenced in this case study, the following websites are highly recommended:

*<www.access.gpo.gov>* (Government Printing Office)

*<www.nara.gov>* (National Archives)

*<www.house.gov>* (House of Representatives)

*<www.senate.gov>* (Senate)

*<clerkweb.house.gov>* (Clerk's Office, House of Representatives)

*<thomas.loc.gov>* (Library of Congress)

*<intelligence.senate.gov>* (SSCI site, the HPSCI does not currently have one)

# ABOUT THE AUTHOR

In her U.S. Air Force career, Dr. Anne Daugherty Miles served as Military Assistant to the Commander in Chief of Pacific Forces and later as Assistant Chief of Staff and Executive Officer to the Commander of First Air Force. She was selected by the Air Force Academy to teach political science, and under the sponsorship of the academy attended Georgetown University, where she earned a master's degree in American government. She taught a wide variety of courses in government at the academy, then was sponsored for doctoral work in political science, again at Georgetown. She joined the faculty of the Joint Military Intelligence College in 1995, where she taught courses in Intelligence and the National Security Policy Process, Congressional Oversight and U.S. Intelligence, and Intelligence Research and Analytic Methods. In 1997, she had the opportunity to serve as a congressional fellow for several months in the office of Representative Tom Davis (R-VA). Lt Col Miles received the JMIC's Beland Award for Excellence in Teaching in 1999. She retired from the U.S. Air Force in 2000. As a civilian, she continues to teach courses as an adjunct professor at the JMIC, as well as at other Washington, DC-area institutions.

# Joint Military Intelligence College

## Occasional Papers

Unclassified papers are available through <*www.ntis.gov*>; selected papers are available through U.S. Government Printing Office <*www.gpo.gov*>.

1. Classified paper.

2. *Getting Intelligence Right: The Power of Logical Procedure*, Capt (USAF) William S. Brei, 1996.

3. *An Office Manager's Guide to Intelligence Readiness*, Russell G. Swenson, 1996.

4. Classified paper.

5. *A Flourishing Craft: Teaching Intelligence Studies*, Papers Prepared for the 18 June 1999 JMIC Conference on Teaching Intelligence Studies at Colleges and Universities, 1999.

6. *Intelligence Essentials for Everyone*, Lisa Krizan, 1999.

7. *Intelligence Analysis in Theater Joint Intelligence Centers: An Experiment in Applying Structured Methods*, MSgt (USAF), Robert D. Folker, Jr., 2000.

8. *Dangerous Assumption: Preparing the U.S. Intelligence Warning System for the New Millennium*, Jan Goldman, 2000.

9. *The Creation of the National Imagery and Mapping Agency: Congress's Role as Overseer*, Anne Daugherty Miles, 2001.

www.ingramcontent.com/pod-product-compliance
Lightning Source LLC
Chambersburg PA
CBHW080833310526
45788CB00020B/3453